450
X

THE
INNER-CITY
CLASSROOM:
TEACHER BEHAVIORS

MERRILL'S

INTERNATIONAL EDUCATION SERIES

Under the Editorship of

KIMBALL WILES

Dean of the College of Education

University of Florida

THE
INNER-CITY
CLASSROOM:
TEACHER
BEHAVIORS

ROBERT D. STROM

The Ohio State University

CHARLES E. MERRILL BOOKS, INC.
Columbus, Ohio

Library of Congress Catalog Card Number: 66-23880

PRINTED IN THE UNITED STATES OF AMERICA

To

Shirley

and

Steven

Contributing Authors

Paul H. Bowman is Executive Director of Community Studies, Inc., Kansas City, Missouri. Dr. Bowman formerly was Director, Department of Preventive Mental Health, Kansas City; and Director, Community Youth Development Project of Quincy, Illinois. He also served as a Professor of Education and Psychology at the University of Chicago, and the University of Louisville (Kentucky). Among his publications are *Growing up in River City*, *Men and Hunger*, and *Mobilizing Community Resources for Youth*.

Gene C. Fusco is a Specialist in School and Community Relations with the United States Office of Education in Washington, D.C. His background includes service as a high school teacher, superintendent of schools, and administrative assistant to the president of George Peabody College for Teachers. Dr. Fusco is past Vice President at Large of the National School Public Relations Association, N.E.A., and an advisor to *Education U.S.A.* His recent publications include *School-Home Partnership in Depressed Urban Neighborhoods* and *Citizens Committees for Better Schools*.

Robert J. Havighurst is Professor of Education, University of Chicago. He is also on the faculty of the University of Missouri at Kansas City as Director of the Study of Metropolitan Problems in Education. Well known for his studies of developmental tasks, Dr. Havighurst began college teaching in chemistry and physics before becoming interested in the problems of education. He has taught at Miami University (Ohio), The Ohio State University, and the University of Wisconsin. The many publications of Dr. Havighurst include *Human Development and Education, Growing up in River City,* and *The Psychology of Moral Character.*

Paul R. Hunt is Director of Federal Vocational Programs for the Detroit Public Schools. Previously Dr. Hunt held positions as Director, Special Education Vocational Rehabilitation Project for Detroit, and counselor in charge of the Metropolitan Job Upgrading Program. He began his career as a high school teacher and has since conducted a number of studies regarding the relationship between student aspiration and preparation for employment. Dr. Hunt has written a number of articles for journals of education and vocational guidance.

G. Orville Johnson is Professor of Education, Syracuse University. Dr. Johnson's professional work started as a teacher of the handicapped. He later held positions as a principal and Director of Special Education before joining the professorial ranks with service to the University of Illinois and Denver University. He directed the New York State Research Project on Severely Retarded Children. Well known for his work with exceptional children, Dr. Johnson has published *Education of Exceptional Children and Youth, Education for the Slow Learners, and Educating the Retarded Child.*

John H. Niemeyer is President of Bank Street College of Education, a center for graduate study and research in education in New York City. President Niemeyer also serves as special consultant to the U.S. Commissioner of Education for the development of training programs for teachers authorized by the Civil Rights Act, and is a member of the Steering Committee of Project Headstart in Washington, D.C. He is past president of the National Kindergarten Association, has been a teacher and school administrator, and writes for national magazines and educational periodicals.

A. Harry Passow is Professor of Education at Teachers College, Columbia University. Dr. Passow serves as Chairman of the College Committee on Urban Education, consultant to Mobilization for

Youth, Inc., research associate at the Horace Mann-Lincoln Institute of School Experimentation, and is a member of the Committee on Educational Disadvantaged Children established by the National Society for the Study of Education. He began his career as a teacher of mathematics and science in high school. Some of Dr. Passow's many publications are *Education in Depressed Areas, Nurturing Individual Potential,* and *Improving the Quality of Public School Programs.*

Elvin I. Rasof is Curriculum Consultant to the Manpower Development and Training Project of the Detroit Public Schools. Dr. Rasof is also a faculty member of the mathematics department at Wayne State University. His principal interests in curriculum, team teaching, and programmed learning have derived from classroom experience at the elementary, secondary, and community college levels in Michigan public schools. He is active as a speaker and has contributed to educational periodicals.

Robert D. Strom is Associate Professor of Education, The Ohio State University. After teaching in public schools located in neighborhoods of low and middle income, he elected college instruction and has since served on the faculties of Purdue University and the University of Connecticut. Dr. Strom recently was Assistant Director of Project School Dropout at the National Education Association in Washington, D.C. Currently, he is Director, the Preface Plan Project. Some of his latest publications are *Mental Health and Achievement, Teaching in the Slum School,* and *The Tragic Migration.*

E. Paul Torrance is Professor of Educational Psychology, the University of Minnesota. Dr. Torrance has been a high school teacher, principal, and counselor. Before becoming Director of the Bureau of Educational Research at the University of Minnesota, he served as a Counseling Bureau Director and as Director of Research in support of Air Force Survival Training. Internationally recognized for his studies of creativity and the psychology of stress, Dr. Torrance is a prolific writer whose recent books include *Gifted Children in the Classroom, Rewarding Creative Behavior,* and *Constructive Behavior: Stress, Personality and Mental Health.*

Preface

The *Inner-City Classroom* focuses upon the extensive, dynamic changes that are developing within our metropolitan areas. This book has been written for those confronted with demands for sound and rapid improvement of our inner-city schools and concentrates on the modification of educational practices which will be necessary to achieve the desired objectives.

Men who support the war on poverty agree that heretofore destitution for a certain element of the population has been irreversible because production was limited, but they insist that poverty in our time is intolerable since cybernation may enable us to produce enough for all. While one group discusses the unacceptable values of low-income people, another group believes there is something more seriously wrong with a societal value structure which does not adequately motivate and educate for useful lives. Whatever the difference in point of vantage, all interested persons will find in this book one vital link in the quest for upgrading social and economic conditions.

The scholars who have contributed to this book have addressed themselves to a concern for improving the education of those who have only recently begun to realize that they can attain greater success and happiness with an adequate education and that men and women who reach adult life with marked deficiencies in learning and motivation will lack prospect. Great changes are already being made as familial support for scholarship is increasing among inner-city parents. Many are expressing concern for improving the schools, and hope is held for gaining better teachers. Considering the various facets of the problem of teaching in low-income areas, the authors have discussed those elements which, when understood by the teacher of inner-city children, will facilitate teacher satisfaction and success.

Subsequent to compiling a list of the teacher behaviors most often cited as requisite to instructional success in schools serving neighborhoods of low income, I contacted scholars who I believe are best qualified to write about these issues. Without exception, their response to the book was positive and, busy schedules notwithstanding, each undertook his difficult assignment. My feeling is that all of the contributors, during their preparation for this volume, realized how easy it is to make an oblique reference to some teacher behavior in a speech but how arduous a task to actually describe such behavior as an author. For their fine contributions, I commend and thank Paul Bowman, Gene Fusco, Robert Havighurst, Paul Hunt, Orville Johnson, John Niemeyer, Harry Passow, Elvin Rasof, and Paul Torrance. I am also grateful to Kimball Wiles for encouraging this venture, to Susan Rohlf for her assistance, and to Shirley for her help and patience.

Robert D. Strom

Columbus, Ohio

Table of Contents

THE

INNER-CITY

CLASSROOM:

TEACHER BEHAVIORS

John H. Niemeyer

Importance of the
Inner-City Teacher

To say that the teacher in the classroom is important—whether the classroom is located in a depressed inner-city area or not—would seem to be a statement of the obvious. After all, if the classroom teacher is not important, who is? School administrators and other supportive personnel play vital roles in a school and a school system, but the critical point in the enactment of the educational program is the point of direct contact with the pupil, namely, the classroom teacher. And this is just as true of an inner-city school as of a school located in the most favored surroundings.

In spite of what seems obvious, there are reasons for exploring the question, for the simple, if unfortunate, reason that many of the teachers as well as other school personnel in inner-city schools are not really convinced that the teacher is indeed important. They would not raise this question at all about teachers in so-called normal classrooms and schools, but they have very serious doubts—often expressed in behavior and attitude even if not verbally—about whether inner-city teachers serve any truly important educational purpose in their classrooms.

The extremes of this attitude are easily discernible. Probably everyone who works with teachers in a relationship which invites

1

confidences has frequently heard comments from teachers such as: "I'm not a teacher; I'm a jailor. Maybe I can do something of value by keeping these kids off the streets and under some kind of surveillance for five hours a day, but that's about the only contribution I make." Sometimes these comments are said with deep bitterness; always they are said with a great sense of frustration and disappointment because of the discrepancy between the teacher's original image of his professional role and what now seems to him to be the reality of that role. To speak to these school men and women about the importance of the classroom teacher in the inner-city school is a mockery.

No one knows what proportion of the teaching body feels this way. Probably the proportion is higher than we would like to believe. For some of those teachers the solution is to obtain a transfer to a different kind of neighborhood as quickly as possible; others simply wait for retirement or resign themselves to a state of professional ineffectiveness and a sense of martyrdom. Still others undergo some experience which causes them to reach out for help to see if there is something, after all, that they might do to change the unhappy situation. One project, involving a large number of schools in the inner city of the nation's largest city,[1] has found that the majority of teachers, principals, and other professional workers do not feel a deep sense of failure such as that described above; but there is no question that a great many of these teachers have serious doubt as to just how important the classroom teacher is.

In fact, this doubt in inner-city schools is such a fundamental and widespread one that we probably must consider it tantamount to belief. This belief is that, while the teacher ought to be of great importance, his effectiveness is largely if not wholly neutralized by the influence of the home, and the influence of the home is considered pre-eminent. But if the school cannot change the homes from which the inner-city children come—and most teachers realize that the school cannot—and if it is believed that the home background precludes the possibility of the school's educating the children effec-

---

[1] The Bank Street College of Education's Public School Workshops, conducted cooperatively with the public school system of New York City, have, since 1943, been located in many of the inner-city elementary and junior high schools, the latest extension of their work being the Educational Resources Center program located in East Harlem and Harlem.

tively, then the conclusion is inescapable that these children, as far as the work of a classroom teacher is concerned, are uneducable. Educators do not like to speak about "unteachables," but there is considerable evidence that the belief that these children are indeed unteachable is widespread. For the statement about the importance of the inner-city classroom teacher to have positive meaning, therefore, something must happen to reduce the sense of helplessness and frustration which teachers and other school personnel feel in the face of the educational problems of the inner-city school.

The Teacher as Part of a Subsocial System

Another reason for questioning the easy acceptance of the importance of the classroom teacher is the extent to which the teacher is limited in exercising control over the classroom conditions. The idea that the teacher operates freely within a learning sanctuary called a classroom is in reality a myth. His classroom is part of a subsocial system known as a school, which in turn is part of a larger subsocial system, namely, the complex of schools established by the community and operated by a school board and its administrative organization. This subsocial system has its written as well as unwritten laws, reward systems, and power structure affecting every unit of the system.

The classroom teacher does not control such factors as class size, the physical plant, the selection of his principal, and the length of the class day. These are obvious influences upon his professional behavior, but there are also more subtle ones. None of these forces is more powerful than the attitudes of administrative and supervisory personnel responsible for rating teachers. An anecdote in a recent best seller (Kaufman, 1964) describing an assistant principal's entrance into the classroom, snapping his fingers at the teacher to stop the phonograph record on which Gielgud is reading Shakespeare, and then announcing, "There will be a series of three bells rung three times indicating emergency shelter drill. Playing records does not encourage the orderly evacuation of the class," may well be an exaggeration. However, when any such attitude toward noise is expressed by someone in power, only the most hardy of teachers will continue an instructional program using audio-visual aids and encouraging talking and activity. Ironically, in college and in-service courses, teachers are taught the importance of audio-visual aids and classroom activities, but strategies for instituting these practices are usually ignored.

It is not only the overt power structure of the schools that influences a teacher's program. The role of the building custodian in discouraging early-childhood teachers from the use of paints and clay in their programs is commonly referred to, although I shall never forget the custodian of one of the New York Harlem schools saying to me, "Look, anything these teachers want to do to help these kids, I'm for. I have two boys of my own, and nothing is too much trouble as far as I am concerned."

The attitudes of a teacher's professional colleagues are an important influence, even if these colleagues have no rating or supervisory power. I have before me a report concerning the teaching of disadvantaged children, written by a teacher of many years' experience who came to study in a Bank Street College institute. This teacher of an upper grade in the most deprived section of a large Eastern city writes:

When I returned to school in the fall I was determined to try out some of the approaches which seemed to work with the deprived boys and girls in the summer school. This was not an easy decision for me, as those of you who had to win me over to try out new ideas last summer can attest. After all, I have been teaching for thirty years. I felt certain that my traditional way of teaching was the only one possible: starting from the first minute making the children remain silent, in their seats, unless given specific permission to move, and at all times knowing that everything they did in class was under my direction. But now, in spite of my tradition, I was determined to try things differently. It seemed clear to me that the boys and girls in the summer program learned to read and speak much more effectively because they wrote and read and talked about things which they knew as a result of the school's providing direct experiences for them. In our fifth grades we are supposed to study early American history. In the past I have simply put the kids through the textbooks, one chapter after the other, with a test at the end of each chapter. Thus I always "covered" the course. This past fall I went to the principal and asked permission for ten field trips for my class in the first three months of school. He looked at me as if I were crazy, but I stood my ground and told him that I had been willing to spend my summer studying new techniques, and now I was determined to give them a try. I got the ten trips! Then I equipped the room with paints and large tin cans in which to mix papier-mâché . . .

The teacher goes on to describe the details of a program for teaching the history and geography of a city rich with early American traditions through the use of firsthand experiences, construction work, experience charts, individual histories written by the children, and information in books. The report concludes as follows:

I succeeded in living with the obvious doubts felt by the principal and his assistant about the messy, noisy program which, for the first time in the history of the school, I was conducting. Now that the test scores in reading show that this year many of my children have gained as much as three years' growth in reading—this has never happened in my class before—I know that I will have the approval of the administration from now on. But I don't know that I will ever win over my fellow teachers. They seemed so upset over what I was doing in the fall that they never missed an opportunity, in the halls or in the teachers' room, to needle me. Needless to say, if I had been more vulnerable, as a younger teacher might be, I probably would never have had the stamina to take the subtle pressure brought to bear upon me from all sides in this school.

In this chapter we are considering the importance not of classroom teachers in general, but specifically of the teachers in the inner-city school. The limitations mentioned above, affecting the professional freedom of the teacher, exist in middle-class schools are well as in inner-city ones. What, then, is the significance of our topic of the controlling influence which the school as an organized social system exerts?

Here we come to the fact that the typical inner-city school is failing to educate its children and youth. Even if we reject the attitude that such a school is only a jail, the truth remains that an excessively large percentage of the pupils in this type of school leave school ill-equipped with the skills, knowledge, and attitudes necessary for reasonably productive lives. If this condition is to change, the school must change. It must provide a different kind of curriculum, group living, and teaching-learning process (Strom, 1965a, pp. 71-95). To be effective, teachers in all kinds of schools need a supportive professional milieu; teachers in the inner-city schools need a milieu which is supportive of change. Unless the inner-city schools change from what they are, the classroom teachers within them cannot be effective educators.

Effecting Change

To bring about change in any large social system is extremely difficult. An extensive discussion of the question of change process in schools and of current research to try to understand schools as social systems seems inappropriate here. A few observations on change process relevant to the importance of the classroom teacher are perhaps in order.

To speak about innovation and change in education has become almost commonplace. There is little agreement about—and as yet little experimentation to discover—the kind of innovation and change (in the formal and informal organizational patterns, rules and regulations, roles, appointments, and rewards within the total social system of the school) needed to meet the tremendous problems of most inner-city schools. Most school board members, superintendents, and principals, if they go beyond calling for better teachers, master teachers, team teaching, or new materials, usually go no further than a shift in school district boundaries and minor changes in the organizational chart of the school's administration. This is not to say that many school systems have not made meaningful innovations. Rather, schools seeking to educate the poor and segregated children and youth effectively require changes much more drastic than most educators think of as desirable or even possible. Henry Saltzman (1963, pp. 322-331) has suggested the community school, involving many agencies, in which the education of children and youth would be directly related to the needs and potential resources of that specific community. Unquestionably, the educational school activities of such experimental programs as Mobilization for Youth, as well as certain aspects of the experimental community-action programs of the Anti-Poverty Program, the extension of Project Head Start, and the application of Title III of the Education Act of 1965, will result in various kinds of new school organizations.

Whatever the future holds as far as new kinds of schools are concerned, there is a current need for existing school systems to incorporate in their operations some mechanism for constantly searching

out ways in which the school system itself ought to change. Bureaucracies, whether of schools or industries, particularly when the
bureaucracies grow large, do not deliberately create key positions
for the purpose of making everyone in the bureaucracy uncomfortable. And it is clear that an "Office for Recommending Change"
would do precisely that. Perhaps the most hopeful solution will be
for school systems to enter into relationships with colleges and universities, and perhaps even non-educational institutions, to establish
cooperating but autonomous change organizations attached to the
school systems.

An experiment in such a cooperative relationship was begun in
1964 by the Bank Street College of Education and the New York
City public school system, resulting in the establishment by the College of an Educational Resources Center in Harlem. The ERC program, consisting of a physical center with curriculum workshops and
demonstration laboratories as well as a professional staff of consul-
tants, is financed by independent foundations and works with the
cooperation of the Center for Urban Education of the Consortium
of Universities and Colleges of New York City. In collaboration with
the district superintendents in charge of schools in Harlem, East
Harlem, and Lower Washington Heights, and with twenty-three of
their elementary and junior high schools, the ERC encourages innovation with curriculum materials and content, teaching methods, and
administrative organization and functioning.

If the teachers are to succeed in efforts to bring about change,
they need continuing support. For the school systems to state publicly that they wish these innovations is not enough. The word "support" must be taken seriously. The pattern which is too often seen
in schools emphasizes this fact. For example, it is not uncommon
for a school system to go to considerable trouble and expense to
interest teachers in new ways of putting life into sections of the curriculum by utilizing short-term institutes, demonstrations by closed
circuit television, and attractively executed curriculum bulletins. All
too frequently, however, when visits are made six months later to
the classrooms of teachers thus encouraged, very little evidence of
the new approaches and materials is found. When questioned, the
teachers usually point out that they started to carry out the new
ideas enthusiastically but then found they had to wait too long for
the materials which had to be ordered, or the new approach led to
noise and what seemed like disorder in the classroom, or they ran

into some other difficulties and did not know where to turn for help, with the result that they finally gave up and went back to their former ways of teaching.

Thus it becomes clear that support for innovation demands that the school systems: (1) ensure that the administrative and supervisory personnel will actually encourage, both formally and informally, the innovation; (2) provide administratively for the easy acquisition by the teachers of necessary materials (how revolutionary it would seem in many systems for individual schools to have petty cash accounts); and (3) make available to the teachers adequate practical classroom guidance over a considerable period of time to help them with their difficulties until they have mastered the new techniques and incorporated the new practices into their total curriculum. All teachers profit by supervisory support; many teachers need it so much that without it they soon give up their effort to make changes which they have been willing, at least, to initiate. In schools where there is a high rate of teacher turnover and a large proportion of inexperienced teachers, the need for such sustained guided support is even more significant (Brickell, 1961).

If this type of curriculum support for the classroom teachers is so important, then it would seem to follow that a high priority should be given to the reorganization within school systems and individual schools of the use of supervisory, or potential supervisory, personnel. Many big city systems have no dearth of professional staff members who are available for this role. Too often, however, these personnel are swallowed up by administrative duties and provide help to classroom teachers only on a crisis basis. Seeing that this type of help for the classroom teacher is available in each school should be the prime responsibility of the principal of the school. To carry out this responsibility, the principal himself must be a learner; he must involve all of his teachers in appropriate ways, and he needs supportive services from the school system at large.

The Role of the Classroom Teacher

The classroom teachers' dependence upon the support of the school does not alter the fact that if the inner-city school is to provide an educational life for children which will help them develop the skills and attitudes necessary for personal happiness and social effectiveness, the vast proportion of the job must be done by teachers in the classroom.

There is no doubt as to the educability of the children, in spite of the widespread discouragement over the inability of the typical school to educate these children successfully. The relative importance of nature and nurture, of innate ability and environmentally-determined ability, continues to be a matter of research, which cannot yet be fully assessed. Whether such a prenatal factor as nutritional deficiency might cause some variation from the normal distribution curve of presumed innate abilities for children of some economically depressed groups is unknown. Certainly all of the clinical evidence which we can observe in our schools suggests that a great many of the children who are so often considered uneducable, when given certain kinds of learning experience respond with a brightness and a learning capacity which seemed previously impossible. My association with institutes which experiment with educational approaches to children who are school failures and who come from highly disorganized home backgrounds has convinced me of the very real learning potential of many of these children. Also, it is possible to go into individual classrooms in schools whose students at the seventh or tenth grade levels are, in the large majority, severely retarded in such skills as reading and see the miracle which is taking place under the guidance of particular teachers. The testimony previously quoted from an inner-city teacher who achieved remarkable results through a different approach to the curriculum is typical of what can be seen in a significant, although still relatively small, number of inner-city classrooms.

It is important to emphasize the additional fact that the successes which can be observed are achieved often with children who have already been in school for at least five years and have experienced only failure in developing the skills which the school has emphasized. The success of the Demonstration Guidance Project in New York City, during the years 1957 to 1962, which served as the pilot program leading to the more extensive Higher Horizons program in that city's public schools, is another illustration. The students selected for this project were considered above average in potential. With the assistance of remedial teaching, adequate individual counseling, and encouragement to work for academic success, a percentage of this group, far beyond the percentage of similar groups in the past, made outstanding achievements through senior high school. What is equally significant is the fact that all of these children, who proved that they were of excellent potential, had already gone through at least six years of schooling without any of this potential being realized. No wonder the authors of the report on the Project conclude: "The program does not call for new discoveries or special techniques, only for thorough education and attention to special needs" (Hillson and Myers, 1963, p. 28). In other words, just by providing some obvious services geared to the needs of children—services which we know how to organize and which would not normally be called innovations—at least the most able of the educationally disadvantaged pupils can be saved from the degree of educational failure which now prevails.

What Is Innovation?

The fact that the methods and the approaches were not new discoveries or special techniques does not alter the point made earlier in this chapter that the inner-city schools must change. There is nothing new about taking students on educational trips, assessing each pupil's academic needs and organizing a remedial program to meet those needs, and counseling as to future educational and job opportunities. But the important fact is that these practices had not been customarily a part of the school program. When they were introduced, therefore, they did indeed represent something new and different. An educational innovation may be something new under the sun. It may also simply be something new in the particular school situation in which it is introduced.

There is no argument against the search for completely new materials, equipment, and approaches. For example, when it becomes possible for a nursery or primary school child to walk over to a corner of the classroom, select a cartridge from a resources shelf, plug the cartridge into a "TV" box, and watch and listen to a color-sound loop describing the growth of a flower, or the functioning of part of his body (only imagination, artistry, and money set limits to the possible topics which might thus be treated), school programs will have gained an important new potential. We need many such new approaches.

Furthermore, many educators who are studying the learning processes of children from unsupportive home and neighborhood backgrounds, children for whom English is a second language, children who have been uprooted from one culture and placed in another, and children from culture groups which have long been alienated, are convinced that there are aspects of the learning problems of these children which we do not understand. These problems may well require techniques and programs different from anything we are currently using.

But the inner-city classroom teacher who sets out to try new approaches, regardless of the degree of support from his school milieu, can feel reassured that there are no esoteric new devices or techniques which he must wait for, and that many important innovations are already known which will enable him to improve the learning of at least the majority of his pupils. Specific effective pedagogical practices vary, of course, with pupil age and other factors. But these practices are known, and they are described in many books on curriculum and teaching; they are taught in many training courses; their rationale has been elaborated by such educational philosophers as Dewey and Whitehead, and such contemporary theoreticians as Biber (1965, 1961, 1959) and Bruner (1960, 1959). The trouble is that in many classrooms these practices are ignored. When the pupils come from education-oriented homes and do not depend almost entirely upon their schooling to open doors of opportunity in society, a reasonable amount of learning takes place regardless of the pedagogy. But when the pupils are from the inner city, the school ignores sound educational practices at its own peril, and the peril of the children and society.

The principles of sound pedagogy can be simply stated. Some of them are:

1. Because meaning can develop only by building upon that which is meaningful, the teacher must always start where a child is—in language, knowledge, understanding, interest.

2. Curiosity and the mastery which results from knowledge are powerful drives for learning built into children, but these drives will operate only if knowing has brought gratification.

3. Because children have different learning styles, teachers should use multi-sensory approaches.

4. Skills are of basic importance, but they should be learned in ways

which teach the child how to continue learning and inspire him to wish to do so.

5. Children learn what they live: therefore, the school should be a small society for each child, in which he is given the opportunity to practice the rational solving of problems, in which he learns that his welfare is dependent in many ways upon the common welfare, and in which he can help in making decisions which actually shape the school society in which he is living.

6. The teacher should act as a model of the respecting, supportive, learning, rational adult, with standards but with no false expectations of perfection for himself and others.

7. Things are seldom what they seem: the wise teacher wonders why individuals or a group act as they do and searches for the real reasons.

The list could be a long one and could be stated in quite different terms. Whatever the items, they need specific examples to be meaningful.

Let us look at the statement, "The teacher must always start where a child is . . ." in light of teaching reading. Many children come to the inner-city schools with a special language which is not the language which the typical teacher expects. But a child's language is his chief symbolic means of communication, and if we wish to have him translate this system from sound to visual symbols, we should start with the elements of his system. A wise teacher, therefore, will use many experience charts, not only to record group stories, her directions to the class, labels of objects and areas of the room, and so on, but personal stories for each child. Using the child's name is the most personal way to start where the child is. Each child can make his own books, illustrated by himself, with the story dictated to the teacher and written exactly as he says it. One successful teacher wrote for a child, "This is a cowboy. He's stopping for a beer." She was showing the child what written words do, without rejecting the language which was natural to this child. She also took photographs of each child, and the children wrote books about themselves. Later she used pupils' names for most of her work on phonics. They liked to sing, so the words of the songs became books. Gradually, written language became an important, necessary tool of communication. And now that publishers are beginning to make real books available which contain written material and illustrations with which these children of the inner-city schools can relate, such a teacher will have textbooks to use once she has established reading on the more personal grounds.

A completely different example of starting where children are is seen in a junior high school experiment in changing the attitudes of a group of underachieving, pre-dropout boys, who were thought to have excellent learning potential. The counselors decided not to start with guidance books or inspirational films, but with the feelings of the boys. Fifteen of them were given a period once a week to meet with two counselors who explained that to try to help them with their teachers they, the counselors, needed to know just exactly how the boys saw the fact that they were failing in most of their subjects. Each session would be tape-recorded, but the tape would not be used otherwise without permission from the pupils. During the first session the boys were vociferous and unrelenting in denouncing their teachers and the school. By the fourth session, however, they were trying to analyze why they as individuals reacted so negatively to school, and why they believed that there was no future for them as poor Negroes and there was no use in making any effort. The role of the counselors was to ask questions that led to a deepening of the boys' analyses. Amazingly, by the sixth session more than half of the boys had altered their classroom behavior dramatically.

Was it the specific technique which made the difference? Or was it the usual Hawthorne Effect? The important truth seems to be that any school practice that starts with the learner will induce learning, and that good teaching must start with what is meaningful at that moment in the child's development. Further, what is true for all pupils may well have special importance for children who have know many alienating forces. Accepting a child's word "beer" without trying to divert the expression to what a middle-class teacher thinks a nice child ought to be talking about may seem like a simple and unimportant incident. Yet it gains deep significance in the light of the following observation of a sensitive volunteer tutor being interviewed about her work with disadvantaged children in an after-school program: "These kids all seem to see themselves in school put down by words, and the words are phoney and they don't care to listen to them. And they see their own words as being unacceptable and probably about something bad that the teacher doesn't want to talk about." Ralph Ellison's advice to teachers is also relevant: ". . . one of the problems is to get the so-called 'culturally deprived' to realize that if they take what we would give them, they don't have to give up all that which gives them their own sense of identity" (Ellison, 1965, p. 47).

Space will not permit examples of other sound pedagogical practices. The fascinating question is why so many teachers, who know at least some of the ingredients of an effective classroom, insist on running their classrooms in such a way as to repress most of the activities and responses which are essential to good education. One reason seems to be a pervasive fear of losing control. Hughes and others have indicated that even in middle-class schools teachers in general spend a major portion of their time keeping order. Deutsch, in a study of inner-city school classrooms, found that the percentage of time devoted to discipline ran as high as 80 per cent (Deutsch, 1960, p. 23). In the forthright terms of a classroom consultant working in a group of inner-city schools: "The idea seems to be to use kindergarten chiefly to teach these kids to sit down and shut up so they can be ready for first grade. In first grade the teachers teach the same things to get them ready for second. In second they repeat it to get them ready for third. And by the third grade the kids don't have the faintest idea of why they're in school, and they're about ready to be incorrigible."

This observation may be unfairly severe, and it would be inaccurate if applied to some of the inner-city classrooms I am familiar with, yet there may well be a connection between its content and Kornberg's description of the junior high school pupils whom the BRIDGE project of Queens College was attempting to reach.

> To use their jargon, they are not "with it." They go through the motions of class activity or remain indifferent to it, finding their own distractions—a few simply putting their heads on the desk and sleeping. With the teacher they are sullenly distant or sometimes shrewdly defiant—and always suspicious. One wonders what has brought this armed truce to so many classrooms . . . But even where ego development is adequate, there is in the classroom a burden that these children can scarcely bear. They have had so much past failure in school that now there is rarely hope for something else. Why try? And besides, the classroom work rarely has to do with what they have experienced or find real. Why listen? (Kornberg, 1963, p. 274).

Now, anyone who has taught in elementary and secondary schools knows that discipline is an important problem facing a classroom teacher. What is written here does not deny this fact. However, there is discipline that represses and limits learning, and there is discipline that creates an order within which productive learning activities can take place with flexibility and freedom. This chapter cannot deal with the many elements of the type of control that supports rather than restricts learning. Some of the critical features are: (1) a program rich in learning tasks which are interesting, meaningful, and achievable; and (2) the ability of the teacher to use the dynamics of the group in arranging a classroom life which makes the execution of these interesting tasks possible. The transfer of a considerable portion of responsibility from the teacher's shoulders to the pupils' depends upon the involvement of pupils in the tasks of the program. Anyone who has ever seen the way children will "police" the production of a play which they have planned and composed—as opposed to the usual behavior when the only motivation is fear of the teacher's reprimand—recognizes the tremendous drive for responsibility which a group of even young children can develop. A classroom in which there are animals to be cared for, pupil-produced bulletin boards, newspapers, interesting books, educational games and puzzles, a science discovery center, a pupil-operated library, and the like, is a classroom which invites children to make decisions, carry out responsibilities, lead, and follow—that is, a classroom in which children can be expected to maintain self-discipline with only a reasonable amount of intervention by the teacher.

One wonders if the prevalence of compulsive concern over control of these children is derived in part from the widespread belief among teachers that their pupils' home and neighborhood backgrounds destine them to be problems. If this is a causal factor, it is indeed ironical, because studies reveal that many of the parents of these children—usually the mothers—look to the school as the only hope that their children may have of a better life than they, the adults, have had. These children, therefore, come to school—no matter how ill-clothed or fed or washed (and many are neatly dressed and well scrubbed)—with just as positive a desire to be good as any group of middle-class children.

Hess of the University of Chicago, in his studies of differential ways in which lower social-class and middle-class mothers teach their preschool children, has discovered that the typical lower social-class parent has said, in effect, to her child when he enters school: "Be good. Do what the teacher tells you," whereas the middle-class parent has said: "You are going to school to learn. The teacher will teach you to read" (Hess & Shipman, 1965). The difference suggests that the teachers of inner-city children need to devise ways of creating for the children an image of the school as a place of learning and of the teacher as a friendly adult whose chief role is to help the child to learn. It also suggests, as do Hess and his associate in the paper referred to, that the school needs to do everything possible to alter the child's learning style from being compliant to authority without any expectation of rationality or of choice between alternatives to a style which is assertive, seeks reasons, and knows how to deal with many alternatives. But it is ironical that the primary concern with the five- and six-year-old children of the poor should be discipline.

Reassuring to teachers who have been led to believe that the children from some families enter school instilled by the home with hostile feelings toward teachers and school, should be the research of Cloward and Jones (1963, pp. 190-216) on the attitudes of differing social class groups. From this research it would appear that teachers in middle-class schools have more reason for apprehension about child attitudes based upon the attitudes of parents. Half the lower-class parents interviewed thought that the public schools were doing an excellent or good job, while only 31 per cent of middle-class parents agreed. Only 19 per cent of the lower-class parents disagreed with the statement, "The teachers here are really interested in the kids," whereas 28 per cent of the middle-class sample disagreed.

The model of the style of teaching and of classroom organization suggested in this chapter as essential if a higher level of learning is to take place in our inner-city schools is quite clearly one in which there is a greater emphasis upon the *discovery method* (Panel on Educational Research and Development, 1964), upon active involvement of children, upon the use of children's interests as starting points, upon the functional use of skills right in the classroom, upon a belief in the innate curiosity of each human being, and upon the teacher's own excitement about learning. This does not mean that there is no important place for drill, the memorization of facts, the learning of information presented by textbook or teacher (Biber,

1965). What is needed is balance, and at the moment our prevalent classroom programs are out of balance because of an almost complete lack of the characteristics of the suggested model.

For the teacher who is willing to move toward the new program, I suggest the desirability of trying out the new approach with a very specific project unit, later fanning out to larger segments of the program.

An example of this step-by-step approach is an inner-city elementary school in which seven out of forty-three teachers volunteered, as a result of an invitation from their principal, to introduce units of the elementary science study curriculum materials with the fifth and sixth grades. These materials (produced by Educational Services, Inc., Watertown, Massachusetts) invite the pupils to explore, to observe, to try out, to record data, to approximate, to construct hypotheses, to test. Pupils work in pairs and must be free to talk and move about. Teachers do not give answers, but record questions and report data, asking questions to lead children to think more deeply or accurately.

The seven teachers were provided with two periods of two hours each during which they worked, themselves, with the units, under the guidance of a science consultant familiar with the new materials. Then they introduced the units into their classrooms. There were many problems. The room furniture had to be rearranged; there was noise; it was not easy to refuse to give the answers when some children floundered. But there was no question about the interest and excitement of the children. Fearing that the class might get out of hand, nearly all teachers at the end of each forty-minute science period returned the room to normal and taught for the rest of the day with the formal, didactic approach. However, by the end of the semester twenty teachers had joined the program and a few were beginning to experiment with the discovery method in social studies and language arts.

This slow approach to a different way of teaching seems to me very wise. By not attempting too much at once, the teachers were never overwhelmed by their problems; it was possible for the principal and the once-a-week consultant to give the needed support, and probably the children themselves were more secure. The important fact, however, is that these teachers and their inner-city school had begun to change in order to make learning a more active, searching, self-directed—and thus more meaningful—part of the lives of these children.

Perhaps lack of meaningfulness in the program is the greatest problem which inner-city classroom teachers must solve if they are to play the important role which potentially they can and should play. Teaching approaches must be directed at this problem; the usual courses of study will have to be drastically modified also.

In the final report of the BRIDGE project conducted by Queens College in part to study the problems of teachers in inner-city junior high schools, the authors write:

> Three years of experience with these underprivileged children convinced the staff that the regular prescribed course of study was not suitable. Particularly in social studies and science there are too many topics, none of which are fully developed enough for the children to comprehend. Consequently, the teachers modified the curriculum, selecting the topics that were most meaningful and supplying the necessary background. They found that the pupils responded well to any topics that dealt with personal relationships. They were curious about their bodies and about problems of race. Like all adolescents, they liked stories of adventure and mystery, but because of their emotional immaturity they also enjoyed fairy tales and fantasy. The teachers learned to become diagnosticians and to take cues daily from the children's responses (Downing, et al., 1965).

Again, the authors of the report, apropos of the interest shown by the pupils in the human body, write:

> The reader may well ask, "Aren't all adolescents concerned with this basic need?" This is, of course, true, but uneducated and impoverished families often lack even the most elementary medical knowledge. Our teachers found that the children had bits and pieces of information—much of it distorted, some false—and some remnants of superstition. They showed an intense desire to get information about all bodily functions, about accidents, disease, pregnancy, alcoholism, dope addiction, and mental illness. They had never had any systematic study of these topics. At the end of the three-year period, when asked on a questionnaire to list the topics they liked best in science, the greatest number of pupils listed the human body (Downing, et al., 1965, pp. 52-53).

A dramatic example of the way in which a young teacher in the project began to see, bit by bit, the relationship between meaning-fulness of content in the school life of these children and their recep-tivity to teaching is revealed in an anecdotal record also noted by the BRIDGE report. During a discussion of the circulatory system of the body, a boy blurted out, "Miss M., what kind of guy is real white, whiter than you? He don't have any blood, right?" Miss M. talked about pigment. The silence was deadening. Then Victoria said, "That ain't true. My mother told us that the reason we is black is . . . Cain was black and Abel white. Because Cain kill Abel, all black folks like us are bad . . ." With the teacher silent, these girls and boys talked excitedly about evidence for this damning thesis. For the first time, the bell ending the class was resented. There would be other biology classes ahead in which the topics of blood and race could be explored but at that moment an explosion of meaning, of significance in the life of the school had occurred. "Since that time," the teacher writes, "I have noticed a delightful freedom in the classroom that was not there before. During math, when we are in small groups, we work and talk. There is a closeness between us that was not there before" (Downing, *et al.*, 1965, pp. 53-54).

Yes, the key to the basic problem of teaching the children and youth of the inner-city school is to achieve meaning, to make school make sense, to create a life in school that can compete with and out-distance the life out of school. It can be done, and whenever the school is even partially successful, the children respond with raven-ous hunger for the food which is offered. But it will never be done as long as the school continues its fetish of covering the course or its idolatry of certain subject matter sequences which have been arrived at through adult "logic." (2 and 2 make 4, it is true, but an under-standing of 2 can be arrived at by first studying 4—or 108!)

For children to develop basic skills in reading, writing, speaking, listening, the use of our number system; for them to have a widen-ing knowledge of the world about them and about themselves as human organisms and as members of groups; for them to have some sense of history, of cause and effect; for them to develop social sensi-tivity and a sense of personal responsibility in society; for them to gain confidence that there are opportunities for those who will strug-gle to find and take advantage of them; for them to gain a beginning of self-perception and release through creative activity, in which I include reading, the arts, physical work, and sports; for them to accept proudly, "I am a man" or "I am a woman"; for them to have a sense of worth, of courage, of love, and a desire to go on learning —how can we as educators say, "We know the sequence, the exact subject matter through which these attributes can be learned?"

Each classroom teacher must put these basic learnings as his goal and then use every means possible to try to achieve them. Am I counseling anarchy? No, because much of the curriculum and resource materials which are not in use or available will serve completely adequately as the mechanism through which the teacher can work—if he uses them not to cover but to achieve the basic goals. I am not afraid of the dangers inherent in the teacher's putting these basic goals ahead of the goals which he or others have written into lesson plans—even if he completely ignores the latter in order to experiment with different programs, materials, teaching techniques (Zacharias, 1965). To continue the educational programs which currently typify the majority of our inner-city classrooms is to march irrevocably toward explosive failure. For the classroom teacher to strive for meaningfulness above all is the only hope through which he can realize the true importance of his profession.

Robert D. Strom

Teacher Aspiration and Attitude

"I'm nobody, who are you? Are you nobody too?"

For a nation of people vitally concerned about maintaining the identity of its individual members, these questions proposed by the nineteenth-century writer Emily Dickinson might be construed as alien to our time. However, for the growing number of persons who comprise America's culture of poverty, the task of becoming *someone* is appreciably more arduous than ever before. Today public acceptance demands that a man be employed; his employer insists he be educated; and his educators require him to manifest school-oriented attitudes and aspirations. Unfortunately, low-income life usually seems to engender a complex of negative factors which preclude the appearance of behaviors deemed necessary for personal advancement and public acceptability.

An encouraging sign is the growing body of research which contends support of educational endeavor is increasing among inner-city families. Bronfenbrenner's review of social-class differences in child-rearing practices over the past twenty-five years concludes that the gap is narrowing (Bronfenbrenner, 1961). Furthermore, Medinnus recently found no significant difference between scores of lower-

and middle-class parents on an Attitude Toward Education Scale (Medinnus, 1962). Across the country one can observe the elevation of aspiration levels among individuals and groups who have been submerged or placed in menial positions over the decades. Their newfound aspirations call for a large share of societal affluence and the education which will make this possible. Underlying the revolution in aspiration and attitude toward learning is a search for a new sense of identity, an insistence upon personal dignity, and an increasing awareness of the importance of schooling as a determinant of life style. Some teachers report they have already noted the positive effect on pupil performance.

With improving familial support of educational programs has come a demand for better schools in central city districts. Claims of the dissatisfied cover a broad range of topics, including student segregation, irrelevant curricula, insufficient materials, and inadequate facilities. A frequently mentioned concern is the lack of skillfully trained, well-intentioned teachers, professionals whose aspirations and attitudes favor instructing children from homes of any economic stratum. Assertions are made that numerous teachers assigned to low-income neighborhoods perceive the job as demeaning, beneath their dignity; consequently they exert little effort to help children, preserve unrealistic academic expectations, and generally disapprove of the families with whom they must work. Support for these assumptions is drawn from the statistical inference that greater rates of teacher turnover, number of vacancies, and incidence of uncertificated staff prevail in slum schools than elsewhere.

Perhaps it is true that few aspire to educate the poor. It is certain that inner-city schools are not the first choice of most teachers. This means many of the recruits for such positions are beginners, persons lacking in classroom experience, who must accept the assignments not selected by their tenured colleagues. Whether they will experience instructional success and personal gratification with their job depends mainly upon the aspirations and attitudes they bring to the classroom (Strom, 1965a). Teacher aspirations serve as the primary criteria for success or failure in the classroom, govern academic and behavioral expectations, and in general, determine methods of instruction. At the same time, attitudes toward the poor affect the motivation of both teacher and pupils, influence objective observation of what is being learned, and provide the base for rapport. Collectively, these factors necessitate an orientation of equity and understanding.

Teaching the Poor

Man's behavior is frequently determined to a greater extent by what he feels than what he knows. Evidence for this thesis abounds in our personal relations as feelings often seem to pre-empt reason as a base for affinity or aversion. Anyone who has attempted to alter the affective response of one person toward another by an appeal to the rational is aware of the strength of emotion and its resistance to logic. Long ago, the French philosopher Pascal recognized: "The heart hath reasons that Reason herself knows nothing of." What once were called *feeling sets* or *reasons of the heart* are known now as *attitudes*. Defined by Allport, "Attitudes are mental and neural states of readiness, organized through experience, exerting a directive or dynamic influence upon the individual's response to all objects and situations with which he is related" (Allport, 1935). Ordinarily, attitudes emerge from firsthand experience, but since each individual cannot know every other individual and because situations arise in which we are called upon to react to people whom we do not know, a common practice is to adopt the feeling of one's in-group, be it family or peer members of race, religion, or economic circumstance.

Apart from the possible danger of adopting attitudes which are unfair, each of us faces the hazard of developing an emotional logic. That is, after sorting people into categories based on their income, color, or other criteria, we selectively admit new evidence about the persons in each category only if the information confirms our previous belief. So a Negro who is dishonest delights certain individuals because he vindicates their prejudgment. It is a pleasure to say, "I told you so." On the other hand, when contradictory evidence faces emotion, one can employ the mental device of admitting exceptions: "There are nice Negroes, but . . . ," or "Some of my best friends come from that part of town, but . . ." This is a disarming device, for by excluding a few favored cases, the negative view is kept intact for all other instances. In short, contrary evidence is not admitted and allowed to modify the generalization; rather, it is perfunctorily acknowledged but excluded (Allport, 1958).

The social fiction embraced by each generation tends to influence the nature of popular attitudes. In our time, myth has it that the urban poor are an unclean, indifferent lot, lacking motivation and aspiration; they are ungrateful people who find welfare an easy form of existence and poverty a satisfactory way of life; a recalcitrant group who evidence no desire to improve themselves, to learn or contribute; an element to be distrusted, feared and shunned. So pervasive is the measure of negative feeling toward low-income families in our culture that it would be strange indeed if such influences did not affect the attitudes of many prospective inner-city teachers. Instructors reared in more favorable environs than the neighborhood to which a work assignment takes them may respond by approaching their job with a sense of reluctance, a lack of desire, a feeling of defeat. For a teacher to so behave is to render a classroom of low-income children immobile; it is to relate academic expectation to economic or racial membership, and thus determine progress before instruction begins. The teacher who feels his job is beneath his prestige expectation will teach down to children, demand unrealistic behavior, or claim that his talents are being wasted even though his dissatisfaction prevents the activation of certain talents. Undoubtedly, when one dislikes teaching, he is difficult to please; his disappointment with his role transfers to children and is reflected in their response. Some children decrease the amount of effort they exert, and others give up after realizing that no matter what they do, neither they nor their work is acceptable.

Expectations and Performance

The preservation of unrealistic goals can affect individual achievement as adversely as teacher discontent with job placement. When stereotypic views thrive, differences among children are obscured. Thus, for those who become preoccupied with the analysis of social class, there is a foregone conclusion that a child's behavior is explained and his personality understood once his economic background is known. For inner-city youth, this is translated into uniform expectations for pupil motivation and performance. The assumption that intellectual homogeneity among pupils exists simply because of a similarity in their economic background is erroneous. In fact, a wider range of individual differences is reported in central-city schools than for institutions located in higher socioeconomic areas. Since teacher expectation is so great a factor in determining success or failure, it requires special consideration.

Despite the higher rates of failure and retention sustained in their schools, a number of educators persist in believing that only lofty objectives will inspire or otherwise initiate the best possible student performance. This hypothesis, defensible to those who argue that high standards must be kept for motivation's sake or that only an extraordinary effort will sufficiently free the child of poverty from his subculture, is not substantiated by current research. To be sure, the group standard which serves as a base for individual progress may motivate some pupils—often only those who can attain its demand. However, for the unfortunate others, those who initially may have tried but were unable to produce at a level above their ability, failure becomes a daily experience that threatens to erode both confidence and academic desire. When one is repeatedly unable to succeed at educational tasks, frustration is expressed in apathy or rebellion as the pupil evolves from dolt to truant to dropout. Smilansky reports that after first grade the ratings of deprived children show marked decrease in their initiative, concentration, responsiveness to teachers, and effectiveness of work habits compared with their behavior a year earlier (Smilansky, 1961, pp. 8-17). The extent of confusion which prevails in all grades regarding levels of expectancy is illustrated in the speech of those who reverently refer to taking a child from where he is to where he should be and in the next breath point out that children from low-income homes are behind when they arrive at school. If one is behind when he begins, it appears illogical to cite the individual as the reference point.

If children fail to exhibit the degree of academic prowess expected of them, it is quite plausible that teacher objectives need revision. However, altering the levels of aspiration for one's students is difficult since the human tendency is to exchange extremes—that is, substitute low goals for lofty ones and to say in effect that the pupil cannot do the work assigned; therefore, he can do nothing. It is imperative to recognize that when student performance indicates levels of expectation might be diminished somewhat, this does not mean expectations are to be abandoned. There is neither strength nor promise for children with teachers who, upon finding their initial expectations of class performance too optimistic, capitulate to no expectations whatsoever. Neither can one sympathize with educators who attempt to assuage their neglect by recourse to rationalization: "These kids are so handicapped now they seem destined to oblivion. Even if I tried, they seem beyond help. What's the use?" or, "I've always wanted more for my pupils in life than poverty has to offer them but my desire to try is depleted as day after day I watch family and community undermine our efforts at school." Equally as disastrous as these manifestations of apathy and resignation in the classroom is the self-deceiving mechanism of projection which allows the teacher to psychologically transfer his own negative behaviors to the pupil's family and neighborhood. However great the indifference of school patrons, no teacher is absolved of the responsibility to care, to strive, and to instruct. Certainly we cannot demand of others what we would deny to them.

There are some disturbing changes that occur in classrooms where high purpose has been replaced by low expectation. One of these is the adoption of a new class orientation. The concern for learning and mental process, consistent with an emphasis on academic behavior, is of necessity replaced by an accentuation of certain physical behaviors. In de-emphasizing mental process and stressing physical behavior, one retreats from a teaching function to a "taking care of" function; the new task becomes one of direction rather than instruction with primary attention devoted to keeping order and discipline. As the teacher is increasingly discouraged with self, purpose, and pupils, a deleterious set of attitudes transfer to the children and soon the instructor is faced with a group of restless students. Then teacher and pupils alike begin to seek a way out.

Teacher inability to modify expectations without sacrifice to instructional quality represents one of the greatest in-school deterrents to pupil achievement. One would assume that educators, ostensibly schooled in confronting change, taught to recognize the need for adjustment, and trained to adapt to the novel and complex, could revise their goals to fit the real situation with minimum difficulty. However, in this context, many instructors seem to fare little better than those whom they are to assist. Whereas it may be easy to explain the economic condition of the poor by citing their lack of educational preparedness and vocational adaptation to a changing labor market, it is not easy to explain why teachers cannot adjust to their task of helping the poor achieve dignity.

The Aspiration Base

There is widespread use of IQ scores as a base for teacher aspiration. Although the intelligence test is certainly not as weak a criterion for predicting academic success as is social class, there are reasons to believe that many major decisions shaping the lives of youngsters will be made solely on the basis of these tests and often these decisions will be dead wrong for individual children involved. Those who oppose current practices of intelligence testing contend that: there is a lack of comparability in the intelligence quotient ratings obtained from tests published by different organizations; most tests are middle-class oriented and therefore distort the image of potential for children in low-income neighborhoods; the tests are too narrow and do not measure the full range of mental functions implied in the term *intelligence*; positive purpose cannot be served when findings are interpreted by the uninformed. In turn, each of these view-points deserves examination.

A common characteristic of intelligence tests is that they yield intelligence quotients. The original Binet tests assessed directly in mental age credits; but most tests today are point scales, the IQ being determined statistically from the distribution of point scores. If these determinations were valid in relation to the definition of an IQ, the distributions of intelligence quotients obtained from the various indices on the market would be alike—they would have the same standard deviation and the IQ's would be comparable. But these standard deviations, rarely published in the test manuals, vary from about 10 to about 26 points; so, a very bright youngster might have, taking the extremes, an IQ of 130 on one test and 178 on another. Or, a child might have an IQ of 80 on one test and be judged a bit abnormal, and score 48 on another and be classified as an imbecile (Good, 1954). To illustrate the seriousness of even a minimal range in dissonance on different test scores, consider the child who, tested between the ages of 8 and 11 under different auspices, had been getting scores running from 130 to 140. According to Stanford-Binet, an IQ of 130 describes the mental ability of one child in 100, while a score of 140 belongs to one in 10,000. The danger of misinterpretation becomes obvious. In order that results obtained from tests produced by different publishers might correspond, an attempt has been made to report scores in terms of *deviation IQ's*. This method calls for conversion to a standard score scale after which outcomes can be compared. Were this practice more common, there would be less difficulty interpreting the many differing IQ's now appearing in the cumulative records of arriving transfer students.

One reason inner-city teachers tend to underestimate the ability of their pupils is because the most commonly administered measures of intelligence seem to engender a *culture load* which favors persons of middle-class orientation. Since the experiences of disadvantaged children are atypical in our society, we cannot expect an accurate picture of the mental abilities for such youngsters to be revealed when using results from ordinary measures of intellect. Essentially, this is the rationale of educators who claim inequity against the poor prevails in testing programs across the country. In response to this currently popular view, a number of school boards acting for urban centers (New York City among them) have discontinued the use of group IQ appraisals and, hoping to find an alternate index of potential, have urged further development of the so-called culture fair tests. When these tests appeared a few years ago, they were called *culture free*, but negative evidence and criticism was so severe that present versions are known as *culture fair*.

Ostensibly, culture fair tests consider the same dimensions of mental functioning as the familiar Stanford-Binet but their distinction lies in exclusion of the language factor. For example, a pictorial approach is used in the Davis-Eells tests for elementary school pupils, generally referred to as the Davis-Eells games. Items found on this test are designed to consider problem solving and other mental abilities which are equally common, realistic, and motivating for every child in our society. Therefore, instead of setting out to produce a series of tasks that could be called culture free, the authors attempted to build in experiential components familiar to youngsters in all income groups. It was believed the test would then be culture fair since performance would not be contingent upon socioeconomic status. Failure of the Davis-Eells tests to eliminate socioeconomic bias is revealed in a number of studies which show that generally the performance of low-income pupils on this test does not vary significantly from their performance on other measures of intelligence (Altus, 1956; Love and Beach, 1957).

Other notable efforts to achieve culture fair measurement include instruments designed by Raven, Cattell, and Goodenough, respectively. Though in an experimental stage with a still deficient normative picture, the Progressive Matrices designed by Raven is a nonverbal test purporting to indicate intelligence by considering the single mental operation of visual perception. The major drawback of this tool seems to be a questionable reliability when used with young children. On the other hand, reliability presents no problem on Cattell's IPAT test (Institute for Personality and Ability Testing). Given to the ten-year-olds in a city of 300,000, the IPAT was readministered fourteen years later to the sample population with no significant differences apparent between either the means or standard deviations (Horrocks, 1964, pp. 271-96). In addition, the IPAT differs from the Raven Matrices in that it does not rely upon a single type of perceptual subtest but includes various types: classifications, mazes, riddles, similarities, wrong pictures, following directions, substitutes, and selecting objects. Many psychologists favor the IPAT over all other culture fair measures. The last instrument for consideration here is the Goodenough draw-a-man test which has received wide recognition in cross-cultural study. Since the human figure is known to every society, it was assumed that various stages of intellectual development might be identified through the drawings children make of man. Although providing sufficient correlation with several accepted indices of IQ, Goodenough's test has been criticized by psychologists who believe that, because of the influence of mass media on children, features of drawing may not proceed today in the same fashion as when the test was prepared some four decades ago. In summary, while culture fair tests do offer promise as adjuncts to our common evaluators of mental functioning, none of the measures in question have as yet become tenable substitutes for the familiar intelligence quotient.

A concern of greater importance than either comparability or cultural bias is the range of mental functions assessed by tests of intelligence. Because educators have supposed the IQ to measure all of man's mental abilities, our concept of the human mind has been limited. Although over one hundred dimensions of the mind have been discovered, perhaps only six of these are considered in traditional intelligence tests: vocabulary ability, general reasoning, memory for ideas, number ability, ability to visualize spatially, and perceptual speed. More significant than the relatively small proportion of abilities that IQ considers is the relative importance of these abilities in today's world. For example, in Guilford's study scientists were presented a list of twenty-eight dimensions of the mind and requested to rank order these in terms of their relevance for successful work in the physical sciences. All but one of the traditional intelligence test factors ranked below twentieth in the list; that is, nineteen out of the twenty characteristics considered by scientists most important on the job were not included in the traditional IQ tests (Taylor, 1961, p. 65). The prospect of this discrepancy applying to other vocations as well as life in general becomes apparent upon the realization that for years educational curricula and materials have been shaped to bring out only the kinds of growth and achievement related to the abilities measured in IQ tests; measures of scholastic achievement have also been patterned along these lines. Moreover, IQ has always been the major instrument used in assessing intellectual potential and mental growth; for determining giftedness and mental retardation; and in some classrooms, the basis for grouping and grading.

What E. Paul Torrance (1965a) and other leading psychologists have been pleading for is a wider view of the human mind, an expanded concept of mental functioning which permits children to learn in creative ways, to use important abilities which are not considered in traditional tests of intelligence. These efforts toward a more humane type of education have been hampered somewhat by the circular logic employed in granting acceptability to new tests. For a test to be acceptable, it must be judged valid; in other words, evidence must exist that the test measures what its authors intend. To establish validity, it has been customary for new tests to show a satisfactory correlation with an existing measure (test) of the same function. The irony here is that no intelligence test measures the composite of abilities implied in the term *intelligence*. When a new test is to be validated, it must measure the identical components of intelligence that the accepted test measures, or validity is lost. Naturally, new tests alleging to measure abilities other than those few called for in traditional intelligence tests may expect low validity. As a consequence, it has been difficult to initiate departure from the narrow definition that "intelligence is what intelligence tests measure." Hopefully, IQ tests, tests of creative thinking, and other instruments will soon be used in combination as indices of potential. Certainly all of our present tests combined do not consider the full measure of man's mind, but in measurement as in all of education we must preserve what is good and work for what is better.

Teachers need to refrain from using the results of intelligence tests as a singular base for expectations in class, for instructional grouping, or evaluating progress (Deutsch, 1964a). The intelligence quotient represents only how well a child copes with a selected group of tasks at a specific time and, therefore, can serve at best as a very rough index of projected school performance when supplemented by tests of other mental functions. In cases where pupil experience has been so deviant or limited that an accurate view of potential is probably unobtainable with a standard test of intelligence, it is advisable to administer one of the culture fair tests as an adjunct to the IQ. Until recently, difference in ability among children was attributed largely to native endowment, while only a modicum of the variation was attributed to the effects of environment. Contemporary investigation demonstrates that for children growing under adverse circumstances, the intelligence quotient may be depressed significantly but intervention at certain periods (especially between ages three to nine) can elevate IQ by as much as 10 to 15 points (Bloom, 1964, pp. 68-76). To increase the prospect of these children is a more worthwhile task than to lament their heritage. The choice rests with the individual teacher.

Classroom Influence

An educator's aspirations and attitudes extend beyond the determination of pupil achievement expectations to markedly influence the province of teacher-learner roles, the nature of interpersonal relations, the kinds of learnings sanctioned and academic behaviors encouraged, the types of lessons assigned and methods of evaluation chosen. So pervasive is the context of a teacher's influence that every area of school life appears affected. As pupil advancement seems so inextricably related to the feelings, hopes, and moods of teachers, it is necessary for us to recognize the manner in which these emotions are mediated in the classroom to foster success or failure.

Where strong feelings urge the adoption of classroom order and control as a primary goal, there is usually an overemphasis on the reactive role of learners; that is, pupil participation is limited to listening and storing away items of information. When the children are allowed to verbalize, their recitation is expected to include only teacher-given data in its original form. Because pupils are required to memorize someone else's learning instead of pursuing their own through inquiry, discussion, and discovery, school lessons are frequently viewed with disdain. To an autocrat, this opposition to education implies the need for further restraints, but in reality it represents an ever-increasing distance between instruction and goals of learning.

To maintain an autocratic classroom in which pupil activity is denied, the teacher must assume the role of an omniscient authority, a mentor who knows all the answers. This task is not only presumptuous but out of step with our time, for being an exemplary teacher no longer implies such a function. To reject this truth is to court insecurity on the job; it requires coveting the active role for self and regarding pupils as reactive organisms; it promotes conditions leading to poor mental health. Under these conditions, the only questions considered valid are those to which the teacher has answers. Indeed, the solo version of catechetical method is often employed as the instructor both poses inquiries and answers them. Pupils that question the reasoning behind certain statements and do not accept the teacher's explanations verbatim are viewed as disrespectful, worthy of suspicion and disfavor. In a needless effort to defend their ego, some teachers label the children whose devotion to inquiry persists as troublemakers. All who would teach need to realize that ignoring the challenge of children is to stunt curiosity, to discourage critical thinking, and to declare healthy judgment off limits.

To minimize discomfort, the autocratic teacher must find ways to rid himself of the intellectual assaults to which he is vulnerable. Apart from developing techniques to circumvent or punish the pupil behaviors which threaten his position, there is a need to justify the limitation of curricula concerns. Often this involves embracing an outdated but convenient form of essentialism which purports that the past is the key to the future and history holds the solution for tomorrow. Therefore, class attention is riveted to pursuing the questions and answers of antiquity. Such a position allows the teacher to remain reluctant about permitting experimentation or discussion, admitting new and different ideas. It also has the effect of setting contemporary motivation off limits, of overlooking the incentive that wonder and inquiry provide. Perhaps autocracy does require less effort since the desires, needs, and values of each pupil do not require attention. But any insensitive and impersonal relationship tends to become a condescending one, alien to conjunctive effort and mutual respect.

On the other hand, the democratic teacher whose attitudes may also be inferred from class procedure recognizes that academic strengths and unique need, interest, and value patterns can be discovered more readily if opportunity is given for a substantial degree of activity and expression. Subsequently, the best way to respect individual differences is to make provision for them by modifying assignments, both in nature and length, to correspond with the capacity of each class member. This eliminates any chance of building discontent and frustration into schoolwork. For instance, slow learners are not expected to encounter the same number of problems as their more rapid peers during an identical span of time; neither is consternation necessary because "Johnny completes his reading too fast and has nothing to do until the others catch up." Also, while autocracy emphasizes conforming response patterns, a democratic approach fosters creativity and seeks to promote learning experiences in which pupils rather than the teacher assume the role of active agent (Torrance, 1965b). This is facilitated in a room where there is ample provision for experimentation, discovery, discussion, and teacher-pupil consultation.

Because the intellectual progress of children is foremost among the secure teacher's in-school aspirations, he does not hesitate to encourage all questions. At the same time, he is not averse to admitting there are questions he cannot answer, ideas he is unable to evaluate. Neither does he consistently greet student inquiry with the reply, "Look it up," as he knows full well that library science is not the only way in which curiosity is mediated. As being responsive to change is requisite for success in our time, the democratic teacher realizes the enormity of his task when facing children whose nurture has led them to believe that fate determines circumstance, they are impotent and cannot adjust, and effecting change is beyond their province. Certainly any attempt to persuade these young people that their judgments can influence the direction of events will fail unless their decisions are allowed to register change in the classroom. To reiterate, teachers must be receptive to pupil thought and opinion; opportunity must be provided for all children to participate in class planning. Only then can boys and girls come to feel a sense of dignity, gain an awareness that their feelings do count, recognize their influence can be felt, and understand that one can alter his own life-space. Offering children less impairs motivation, limits the number of students who are really concerned about what happens in the classroom, and reconfirms the message of fatalism.

Interpersonal Relationships

Many writers contend that until class size is reduced in low-income schools, teacher-pupil rapport will remain impersonal and cannot be expected to improve appreciably. It is true that impersonality implies inattention and, therefore, classrooms so oriented are inimical to achievement. However, as impersonality is more contingent upon teacher attitude than teacher-pupil ratio, it seems feasible that impersonal responses may be diminished apart from a decline in pupil membership. Certainly excessive classloads are undesirable as they enlarge the task of knowing all children. But during the interim, until reasonable ratios are forthcoming, each of us can alter certain types of impersonal associations which, though often inadvertent, are damaging. We are impersonal when we let grade or age norms determine our expectancy of how children should think, speak, feel, and act. We are impersonal when the norm dictates just how much Johnny can absorb and serves to classify him as a potential failure or success before ever becoming involved with him. We are impersonal when IQ is allowed to determine whether a child is to receive respect or be held in low regard. We are impersonal when we avoid familiarity with students on the premise that a close relationship might destroy the objective base for grading. We are impersonal when we remain insensitive to situations which damage self-concept, such as asking pupils to publicly announce their grades in order to facilitate our task of recording marks, subjecting children to public failure at the blackboard, or sanctioning the archaic "spell-down" in which winners are predetermined and losers are singled out for embarrassment.

Impersonality can be observed in class discussions where parataxic relations exist. This happens when a youngster's comment is halted on the insulting assumption that we know what he is going to say before he says it; or we prematurely interrupt a student on the premise that his response is irrelevant. Such a "mind reading view" fails to recognize that for most children, and especially those of low income, answers may begin with what we as adults consider extraneous information before the pertinent data is given. Bear in mind that a child's supposedly irrelevant preamble to those answers we seek may be germane as seen from the youths' view. Unfortunately, we allow the tyranny of time and scheduling to prevent some students from making their thoughts and opinions known. This problem is extended in classes where transaction between students is limited, when instead of encouraging interpersonal relations, situations are constructed which isolate children by forbidding them to talk or collaborate. Because our system is founded on competitive grades, pupils are expected to refrain from talking or seeking information from others since this is construed as cheating (Conner, 1965). In these ways, boys and girls are denied the prospect of learning from interaction with their peers—this in an era when major contributions to society will require conjunctive effort by persons of different backgrounds and persuasions. Finally, examples of impersonality are replete in grouping practices. If selection of membership for instructional groups is based on the differences teachers see among children, why are so many instructors unable to see more than three kinds of youngsters, usually tagging them with subtle but descriptive terms like the steamboats, rowboats, and barges. Separately, the concerns mentioned here are perhaps minor. Yet collectively they constitute an impersonal environment, a classroom in which the value of the child as an individual is ignored.

The result of impersonality is that one cannot transfer motivation to children; the vehicle of personal enthusiasm with which to inspire others is lost and with it the chance to improve pupil self-concept. Brookover's research indicates that as self-concept is elevated, pupil achievement tends to rise; the converse follows when ego deflation occurs (Brookover, 1964). Whether feelings of adequacy or inferiority are developed seem to depend in part on the nature of teacher-pupil relations. Students sense whether they are viewed as valued persons by the way an educator communicates concern and regard. Therefore, the effective teacher listens to his students, to what they say and what they are trying to say, perceiving the Victorian admonition, "Children are to be seen and not heard," as an inappropriate guide for modern classroom management. Further, even though it is difficult to understand how content which appears relatively simple cannot be grasped readily by all students, the good teacher combines patience with perseverance; he instills confidence by respecting each child; he makes the "help process" a personal one.

Homework and Evaluation

The conditions under which homework is assigned reveal much about an educator's perception of the teaching role, the role of the learner, and the nature of learning. To use out-of-school assignments as a punitive device for reducing misbehavior in class is hazardous, for one runs the risk of jeopardizing all attempts designed to inculcate a desire for learning. Just as irrational is the procedure which requires pupils to read a certain number of pages or complete extra problems at night because they were unable to produce the acceptable amount or quality of work during school hours. Underlying this judgment is the teacher's feeling that such students need more practice, that the discipline of finishing tasks will develop personal responsibility and culminate the learning process. However, for children who lack the understanding to successfully finish work, additional drill will only serve to frustrate. If drill is to be effective, it must be preceded by meaning. Otherwise, having homework does not necessarily mean one is learning more; it means only that he has more to do.

Perhaps the greatest weakness of homework today is the lack of a constructive purpose. In the main, teacher attention is devoted solely to the student's finished product or answer rather than to considering the processes used to derive solutions. Instead of diagnosing why a pupil is making errors, the expedient goal is to be content with numbering his mistakes. In other words, achievement classifica-

tion seems more central to the homework objective than does a de-
tection of error type or the correction of inappropriate process. Also
of importance is the fact that while many children when in doubt
about aspects of school instruction have recourse to competent parental assistance, this help is usually unavailable to low-income children. Indeed, schools can undermine the respect students have for
parents when the latter are faced with the precarious task of having
to explain lessons which are beyond their comprehension. In any
case, when the homework product rather than process occupies
teacher attention, pupils become eager to finish and may resort to
inaccurate shortcuts, thereby defeating the only tenable aim of the
assignment. For students to whom completion has become a compul-
sion, there is a tendency to equate achievement with that which one
has finished. If problem solving is the goal of most homework activity, then its substance, which is method, should receive careful evaluation. If this is not the case, the lesson is uninstructive; it cannot
be diagnostic; it is without positive significance.

A stated purpose of evaluation is to assess academic gain. When
the real purpose is in conjuction with this stated intent, numerous
examination types are utilized in order that students of differing
learning styles and strengths may be afforded an equal chance to
perform. In contrast, when recall and recognition tests dominate, as
they often do, youngsters are denied an opportunity to demonstrate
their prowess in circumstances requiring critical thinking, problem
solving, and decision making. There is reason for concern about the
dissonance between behaviors teachers verbally encourage and those
behaviors actually rewarded in the test situation. The role of hypoc-
risy is enacted for students if we characterize our age as one in
which problem solving is vital and then prepare examinations designed exclusively for memory orientation. Equally unfair is the
structuring of assessment contexts which penalize the poor. As
choice and option are foreign to low-income experience, these children find tests requiring the selection of a correct response from
numerous alternatives to be especially difficult. As the number of
options increase, the reticence to choose is more obvious as is the
quandary of deliberation. For some pupils, the number of unfinished
multiple choice items on timed tests would seem to suggest either
less questions should be included or more time should be provided.
We can conclude that if the attitudes a teacher maintains are ex-

pressed in unfair measures of evaluation, learning will be disrupted and mental health impaired. These costs are too high to disregard.

The prevalence of fluctuating extremes in the achievement expectations of teachers leads to evaluative practices which are both inaccurate and incomplete. Beginning instructors who typically seek assurances regarding their capability and level of performance represent a prime example. Ordinarily they select some global index by which instructional effectiveness can be gauged, usually class progress over a short period of time as measured by teacher-made tests or observation. Needless to say, the desire for quick academic breakthroughs seldom occurs. One must then face the reality that a great deal remains to be done to help these children or one can activate defense mechanisms by projecting a cloud of failure onto the students. Perhaps we facilitate this projection by describing children from low-income homes with adjectives like underpriviledged, culturally deprived, and socially disadvantaged in that, although the referent is their environmental limitation, the terms tend to create an image of less potential. Misfortune has several dimensions here: it is not just that failure to achieve the improbable should so affect teacher perception of pupils or self; neither is it the ready adoption of a new extreme in achievement expectation. It is the use of myopic observation so constricted as to prevent one from seeing that which he ostensibly seeks.

To view change in measured achievement as the singular criterion of progress is to overlook other equally important changes in pupil attitude, academic behavior, and orientation. Additional aspects of developmental change that need to be viewed as signs of progress include the valuing of educational endeavor, finding pleasure in learning, the ability to attend to others and engage in purposive action, gains in the ability to delay gratification of desire and to work for goals which are more distant, the viewing of adults as sources of information and ideas, and also as sources of approval and affection, and the adoption of a future time perspective (Bloom, Davis, and Hess, 1965, pp. 12-19). As these behaviors represent the foundation of academic achievement, it would be a mistake to ignore their importance or fail to credit their growth.

In conclusion, whenever the poor and their problems are discussed, one may expect to hear, "Who is responsible? It certainly isn't us. We in management have our duty and that is to make a profit; we in labor have our jobs and that is to ensure every working man a fair deal; we in government cannot get very far ahead of the people; we in the churches have a redemptive mission; we in education already have a running system" (Theobold, 1964). Yet someone must lead; someone must initiate effective measures to render possible the escape of millions who find themselves victims of an environmental trap. If a new moment is to come to birth in our time, a moment which promises freedom from want and hunger for all, it is essential that the quest for learning be elevated to a position never before realized. Schools can help make it so if they maintain curriculums that are interesting and relevant; if they respect differences in learning style and pace among pupils; if the aspirations and attitudes of teachers favor the growth and well-being of every child.

Robert J. Havighurst

Overcoming Value Differences

The Samuel Slater School* is an elementary school located in an area of *de facto* segregation in a large northern metropolitan city. Because of the residential patterns, seventy-one per cent of the school population is Negro, the remainder almost all Puerto Rican. Mr. Fields, the principal, had worked in this area for fourteen years. Each year he had faced the problem of teacher turnover. In the fall of 1964, fifteen new, totally inexperienced teachers, newly graduated from college, had been assigned to the school. A man in late middle age, with grown children of his own, Mr. Fields prided himself on his fatherly approach to the new teachers. He had become increasingly aware of the need to help them toward a better understanding of the children with whom they would be working, and the community in which they would be working.

Mr. Fields anticipated that, with rare exception, his new teachers

---

* This incident is taken from: *Pickets at the Gate* (1965) by Estelle S. Fuchs, Hunter College of the City University of New York. This is a production of Project TRUE, directed by Marjorie B. Smiley and aided by a grant from the Office of Juvenile Delinquency and Youth Development of the United States Department of Health, Education and Welfare. (Reprinted by permission.)

would be young white women who had very little, if any, firsthand acquaintance with conditions in a Negro and Puerto Rican neighborhood. Their student teaching experience would probably not have included working in a school of this population, and even if it had, such experience is widely known to be a sheltered, relatively artificial one. Many of the new teachers, he was certain, would never have worked with Negro and Puerto Rican children. He believed, because of past experience, that many of the new teachers had grown up in middle-class white communities and had little acquaintance with people outside of their families and college friends. He assumed that many had never been exposed to poverty or the breakdown of family to be found in the community to which they had now been assigned.

He had been reading a great deal concerning the characteristics of children in depressed areas. Finding the materials very interesting, he felt that they would be of value to his teachers. Thus, in an effort to cushion the shock he felt the young teachers might suffer upon meeting the children of this community, he sent the following letter to his faculty:

Welcome back from vacation time. I hope that you have recharged your batteries and are ready for the challenges of the coming academic year.

Some of you are younger and more spirited than your older colleagues. It is to you that this letter is primarily addressed. Your more experienced colleagues can corroborate what follows:

Our school receives many special services such as smaller registers, more money per child, and teacher specialists. Why do we get these special services?

Our children, for the most part, come from homes that are usually disadvantaged. That means that, compared with middle-class homes, they are poorer financially, academically, socially. Specifically, many of our children are on welfare. We serve over 500 free lunches daily. The school lunch is the best meal they get.

Many of our children have no father at home. There can be no organized family activities. There is lacking a male image. The mother is so busy with her brood that the individual child is lonely. He has no conversation with the mother or other adults. He is unaccustomed to listening. In fact, living in a noisy atmosphere, he has a higher hearing level, i.e., he shuts out most noises and sounds in self-protection. Hence he is not going to hear his middle-class teacher who speaks quietly until he has been trained to do so by his teacher who has this as one of her conscious, specific aims.

The language he hears at home may be Spanish. Or it may be the speech of a parent who is illiterate or of limited schooling. The Spanish child knows that his parent does not speak English so he is more likely to imitate his teacher's speech. The other child acts on the assumption that his parent speaks English and hence is less likely, possibly, to imitate the teacher. An intense attention to correct speech by your children is most essential.

Furthermore, there is lack of encouragement at home to achieve. There may be absent adequate male models. Families on welfare for the third generation lack academic drive.

The physical situation at home may be deplorable. Cold flats, no hot water, peeling paint and falling plaster, vermin, overcrowding—these are the characteristics of the homes of some of our children. For such children, school is an oasis from squalor. You will find that your attendance is highest on the coldest days, for school is clean and warm.

Coming from a poor environment, socially, culturally, economically, physically, it is no wonder that our children are not ready for school when they enter and that, in the case of some of them, there is a cumulative decline in academic achievement as they move along in a school whose staff is middle class and whose values confuse some of the children. Specifically, the proper care of textbooks, the keeping of an accurate, neat, complete notebook, punctuality, proper dress and cleanliness are things which we have to teach the children, and, unfortunately, some parents. These are characteristics of poverty irrespective of ethnic groups. The people of the Appalachian Mountains, the Ozark hillbillies, the Mexican-American migrant farm workers, have these attributes as well as poor Negroes and poor Puerto Ricans.

One purpose of this letter is to help you rid yourself of certain misconceptions: not "all slum children are slow learners." Actually, "underprivileged kids have just as wide a range of abilities as middle class kids" (Professor A. Harry Passow at Teachers College). Hence, you must not have the idea that your role is chiefly custodial. That if you keep them quiet and in their seats that you have earned your salary; you haven't. Mere custodians are taking their checks under false pretenses. You have a license as a teacher. That is your job—to teach—to teach with all these difficulties in mind, to try to compensate for their handicaps. If you are indifferent to their academic achievement or lack of it, they will continue to be indifferent to their poor environment, and minority group status is not their fault. Nor is it yours. But it *is* your responsibility to plan your work with these facts in mind.

What are you going to have as your basic goals? Of primary importance is social living. Unless your class has real discipline, not authoritarian order, you don't have a real teaching-learning situation. We line the children up quietly. They go into the building quietly; they go to your room quietly. Then, it's up to you.

Your first days will be devoted to training in routine; mechanical aspects of the classroom must be mechanized. You will see to it that the children are clean, that every child's hair is combed, and that every boy has a necktie on.

There are certain basic academic skills that you will stress. These are:

1. Listening
2. Reading
3. Expression of ideas
4. Mathematics

Your "School Manual" has specific suggestions for these and other areas. Read it. Consult it. Don't let it gather dust. Use it in preparing at home. It is easier to prepare interesting lessons at home than to fight a disciplinary situation resulting from boredom with an uninteresting lesson.

Through our PTA we are going to try to instill a greater sense of responsibility in some of our parents. We will try to get them to understand the importance of:

1. Cleanliness
2. Proper dress
3. Punctuality
4. Attendance—unless ill
5. Care of school property
6. Neat, clean, complete, accurate notebooks
7. Academic achievement

From you the teachers I expect:

1. Punctuality
2. Careful preparation
3. Functioning on a level above that of the children
4. "Know how to call to the man which has lain dormant within the soul of the child."

There are many other things I could say, but this letter is much too long already. Hence, I shall say no more at this time.

But I do pledge you on behalf of the three supervisors our complete cooperation and aid. Their activities will be not only in the school, but in the community at large too, for there are certain responsibilities that the community must assume and not purge itself of a sense of guilt by criticizing the schools.

Mr. Fields, wishing to let the parents know how the school was helping new teachers do a better job, sent a copy of the letter to the president of the Parent Teachers Association.

At the PTA executive board meeting held that week, Mrs. Post, the president, reported the communication from the principal. She was somewhat apprehensive about doing so because she felt the letter had been unwise and she wished she could have discussed it with him before the meeting. Upon reading the letter, several members of the board immediately became infuriated. They viewed the letter as insulting, degrading, and designed to hurt their children. Although the executive board took no official action at this time, largely because of Mrs. Post's urging, discussion and anger at the principal became the subject of the entire meeting, and an unofficial committee was formed by several executive board members to see the principal to demand an apology.

When the committee called upon him, Mr. Fields was absolutely astonished. Indignant at what he considered an unjustified response by the parents to his sincere efforts to improve the school, he informed the parents that he had intended no harm and saw no need to apologize.

Angered by the principal's refusal to apologize, the parents' committee began to circulate the following petition in the neighborhood of the school calling for his ouster:

On September 11, 1964, Mr. Fields, Principal of Slater School, issued a letter to the school teaching staff in which he made the following comments about our community—our parents—our children:

 a. "compared with middle-class homes, they are poorer financially, academically, socially"
 b. "many of our children are on welfare . . . the school lunch is the best meal they get."
 c. "the mother is so busy with her brood that the individual child is lonely."
 d. "many of our children have no father at home."
 e. Our children are "living in a noisy atmosphere."

f. "there is a lack of encouragement at home to achieve."

g. "Families on welfare for the third generation lack academic drive."

h. "Coming from a poor environment, socially, culturally, economically, physically, it is no wonder that our children are not ready for school . . ."

i. "the people of the Appalachian Mountains, the Ozark hillbillies, the Mexican-American migrant workers, have these attributes as well as poor Negroes and poor Puerto Ricans."

Do these comments accurately describe you and your family? We deplore these intemperate, injudicious and uninformed remarks. They speak more to the discredit of Mr. Fields than any of our families. We contend that these remarks represent Mr. Fields' attitude toward us and our children. The image he presents is insulting, inaccurate and detrimental. No school can thrive under this calibre of leadership. Indeed, Mr. Fields refused, when asked by parents, to apologize.

We, the undersigned, demand the removal of Mr. Fields from the principalship of Slater School.

This actual incident can help us to understand the complex matter of differences between the school staff and the parents and children of a socially disadvantaged section of the big city. It is an oversimplification to say that the problem is due to differences in values. The parents who objected to Mr. Field's letter did so not because they had different values from Mr. Fields and his staff. They did so because they *share* values with Mr. Fields and are angry because he is critical of their performance as parents. But it is also overly simple to say that the parents and Mr. Fields have the same values. There are some value differences, and these need to be understood by the teacher.

The Gaps Between School, Parents, and Pupils

What are the differences between pupils and school staff that cause difficulty for the inner-city school? What are the differences between school and parents (as reflected in pupil problems and behavior) that cause difficulty in this type of school?

These differences can best be seen as *gaps between the school and the pupils in knowledge, skills, and values.*

The knowledge gap and the skill gap are there mainly because the pupils are immature and have not had enough time and experience to acquire the knowledge and skills they will need as adults. Everybody understands that the teachers' job is to help their pupils to close the knowledge gap and the skills gap that exist between the pupil and the teacher. Pupils are expected to learn, teachers are expected to teach. That is what the school is for. Parents understand this, no matter where they live and what their incomes are.

The Value Gap

More difficult for people to understand and cope with is the value gap between school and pupil. This is partly because the values which the pupil should learn are not so clearly understood and stated in the school curriculum as are the knowledge and skills he should learn, and partly because there are subtle or not-so-subtle value differences between the parents and the schools. Where the parents and the schools differ in values there is a competition between parent and teacher that does not exist in the area of knowledge and skills. The poorly educated parent recognizes that the teacher is a better reader, speller, and master of arithmetic and history, and expects the teacher to help his child become superior to him. But he does not recognize so clearly that his child may become superior to him, in certain values, with the aid of the school.

A value is a state of affairs or a thing that is desired by someone. Some of the values that the American school must teach if it is to be successful with its pupils are:

Punctuality.
Orderliness.
Conformity to group norms.
Desire for a work career based on skill and knowledge.
Desire for a stable family life.
Inhibition of aggressive impulses.
Rational approach to a problem situation.
Enjoyment of study.
Desire for freedom of self and others.

These are values of an urban, industrial, democratic society. *They are not social class values*. It is misleading to speak of the school as a protagonist of middle-class values versus the inner-city homes and neighborhood as a nourisher of lower-class values, with resultant conflict. This talk has just enough basis in fact to worry an inexperienced teacher, but not enough to serve as a basis for a positive educational program aimed at reducing the value gap.

A young Negro woman high school teacher had the following to say:

> I want you to know I took time out of a very busy weekend to talk to you because I felt someone should know what is going on at our school. The violence and stabbing between the students, not the teachers but the students, is getting worse every day. In my opinion, this is taking place because of the weak position taken by the principal. We are now on our third principal in two years. The others were moved up to supervisory positions, I believe. The last two were Negroes, the first one was white. In every instance, the principal did not want to come to grips with the violence of the students. He might be blamed and that would stand in the way of his promotion. So it was better to ignore it and leave it up to the next principal. Since the students recognize the changing and weak administration, they feel there is no control over them, and they are getting out of hand. The climate is one of fear and intimidation, particularly of those students who want to learn. I don't know how anyone can learn in such a climate.
>
> These students have so many problems—home problems, personal problems, school problems. In many instances, there is no authority that they respect. And here at the school, this carries out exactly what's been happening in their home. In the past two years, I've had two students who tried to commit suicide. One was an honor student who had won a scholarship, but she found herself pregnant, and no one was aware of it for five months. And then, when she couldn't conceal it any longer, she tried suicide. I had another student, just a few months ago; I was having some problems with her, and I asked her mother to come into the school. I didn't know that her mother had just come out of a mental institution. This child was trying to conceal it, so while the mother came to the school, the child took pills at home in an attempt to commit suicide. I feel almost responsible here and have been involved with the whole situation ever since. You can't help but become involved, and you can't help but stay involved.

This young woman was not talking about a conflict of social class values. She was talking about a disorganized, demoralized community in which the pupils want to do better but do not know how, and the parents do not know how to help. In this community it is not the school with value set A working against the neighborhood with value set B. It is the school without a coherent and effective set of values and without good leadership working in a neighborhood without a coherent and effective set of values. If the school were to state explicitly a program for teaching some such set of values as those listed above, and were to organize itself for this task, most of the parents in the neighborhood would support the school to the best of their understanding and ability.

The value gap between the inner-city school and its parents is an ill-defined set of differences which nobody has tried to define clearly enough to be able to mount a program to reduce or bridge the gap. However, experienced teachers have learned to bridge this gap with at least some of their pupils. For instance, a woman who has taught for more than thirty years in a slum school said:

> You know, there's a lot more to school than just the teaching of reading, writing, and so on. There's your character building and your socialization, citizenship, and so on. There are those lessons that you try to teach, too. I have always tried to give my children ideas like that of sticking to things until they are done, not giving up.
>
> I remember I had a boy, a good many years ago, who wasn't very bright. He was in the low eighties, I think, as far as intelligence went; well, he had his heart set on being an architect. Here the poor fellow could barely read and he wanted to be an architect. Well, I gave him all the encouragement I could. I didn't think he would finish grammar school, but he did it, and went on to high school, too. Then I lost track of him. Well, not too long ago, as I was leaving school, I saw an enormous truck standing outside of school. Just a great big old thing, you know. I was standing looking it over and I noticed a name on the side of the truck. Just then this boy came up, a tall gangling thing, now. I said, "How are you, Edward?" He said, "How are you, Mrs. _____? What do you think of the truck?" I said, "It's certainly a fine truck. But I notice your father's name down here. I thought your father was dead." He said, "Oh, Mrs. _____, he is. That's my truck. I've got three more just like it." He'd gone into the trucking business and made a wonderful success at it. I always knew that he would get someplace if he tried, because, though he wasn't terribly

smart, even in grammar school he had the most beautiful manners. He was so suave, so diplomatic always. He said, "Yes, Mrs. ———, you used to say something in your classes that I really took to heart. You used to say that the important thing was stick-to-it-tiveness. Well, I thought about that a lot. And I did stick to it. I was in high school before I realized that I didn't have what it took to be an architect. But I knew that no matter what I went into I would need a high school education. So I stuck it out. And I never regretted it, either. I went into the trucking business and, do you know, Mrs. ———, I'm making a pile of money in it. I always followed your motto, 'Stick to it.' It really helped me."

There are other value gaps between the school teacher and pupils in various types of schools. For instance, a teacher may have great interest in critical and lively discussion, and wide reading, and may set a high value on self-directed effort by pupils, with less value on the more routine drill that is a part of the school program. This teacher will be happy in one type of neighborhood and uncomfortable in other areas where the parents and their children do not share her intellectual values. For example, a woman of this type taught for her first few years in the Q——— school, which had mostly Jewish children who were keen to learn and kept the teacher on her toes. Then she transferred to the K——— school, in a disadvantaged area, and after fourteen years at K———, she transferred to the Y——— school, in an area of the stable middle-middle class people. She comments:

I taught at the K——— school for fourteen years. That's located in a very underprivileged neighborhood. Very underprivileged. I finally transferred from there after fourteen years. It wasn't that I couldn't get along there. It was just that I felt that I couldn't accomplish anything there. I was very discouraged. I never seemed to reach those children, you know. It was so hard to get them interested. And so few of them ever really tried to get what you were trying to put across. It was hard, and unrewarding, if you see what I mean. You had to go over and over things, and then only to see half the class miss the point completely. You didn't feel as though you were accomplishing anything. You couldn't see any results. You'd work and work, and then you just couldn't see any results from your work. It was very disheartening. So I finally left there. Not because I didn't like the neighborhood or the children or anything like that. But because

I felt I really wasn't accomplishing anything there. I couldn't do my best work there with those children; I felt as though I should be working some place where I could do the best job that I was capable of. I couldn't do it there. Those children were just extremely hard to teach—poor things! And, after all, I'd been there fourteen years. That's a long time. I figured I had done my bit for humanity and my fellow man. So I felt that I deserved a chance at something else.

I transferred out here to the Y——— school. It's a very nice school. And, I'll tell you the truth, I'm a little disappointed. See, you might say that the reason I left K——— in the first place was that I was looking for more teachable children. Well, I didn't exactly know what I hoped for, but they're not it. They're not like the children at Q——— that I knew. Y——— contains what are probably middle-group Scandinavians. You see, these children are mostly Swedish and Norwegian and they're kind of dull. Well, not dull, that's not fair, but they're slow, you know. They don't respond too quickly. It's not like the Jewish children at Q———. You know how they are—eager to learn all the time. These children aren't like that at all.

These examples of value gaps are enough to indicate that the task of overcoming value differences is not simply one of missionary work in a value-hostile territory. The values to be taught are those that make for competence in an urban, industrial, and democratic society. Most of these values are given lip service, at least, by parents at all socioeconomic levels. Often the parents of the inner city have been defeated in their awkward attempts to achieve these values and they do poorly in teaching their children. The school can and should teach this set of values explicitly and positively, counting on a good deal of parental support from a substantial group of families. Schools and classrooms can be organized so as to do this job.

Expressive and Instrumental Cultures of the School as Sources of Value Learning

The school generally seems best fitted for closing or reducing the knowledge and skill gaps between pupil and teacher, and for reducing the value gap on values which are those upheld by the organization and functioning of the school, such as the value of enjoyment of reading, the value of postponing present gratification in favor of future achievement, and the values of punctuality and of conforming behavior. Thus the school tends to be successful in teaching certain values to pupils who learn the school knowledge and school skills readily.

But the school has two cultures—an instrumental and an expressive culture. The instrumental culture of the school consists of the activities which lead to the knowledge, skills, and values that are stated to be the objectives of education. A pupil studies and learns for the sake of something outside of and beyond the process of studying and learning—to be promoted, to be praised by his parents, to get a diploma, to become a good citizen, to become a competent lawyer or carpenter. The school consists of a set of instrumental procedures which produce a person who is a reader, a writer, a master of a foreign language, a mathematician, etc.

The expressive culture of the school consists of the activities which pupils and teachers take part in for the sake of the activity itself, rather than for some goal beyond the activity. Thus the playing of games at recess and after school are part of the expressive culture of the school, as are the annual celebrations of Christmas, Valentine's Day, Easter, and May Day. So are the parties, and much of the music, the school lunch, and the school prayers, if prayers are said.

Although the expressive culture of the school sometimes involves the learning of skills and knowledge, these are generally not so important as they are in the instrumental culture. A child can enjoy singing in a chorus, or playing on a class team, or celebrating a holiday, without learning much of skill or knowledge. Also, the instrumental culture sometimes has expressive aspects, as when a child learns to love to read, or learns to enjoy solving arithmetic problems and will do those things for their own sake. There is an instrumental undertone to most expressive activities, and an expressive aspect of most instrumental activities. But the pupil generally distinguishes the expressive from the instrumental culture.

The expressive culture is good for teaching values, since most pupils can succeed in the expressive culture and there is not such severe and explicit competition as there is in the instrumental culture. Thus a pupil can learn to like school, and to value punctuality and conforming behavior through successful participation in the expressive culture as well as in the instrumental culture. Also, the parents can generally be involved in the expressive culture and can thus learn some of the school's values.

There are various combinations of success and failure in the expressive and the instrumental cultures of the school, and the child's social and intellectual development depends on his particular combination. A high-high combination in both cultures is characteristic of the good student who is somewhat of a leader and grows up to be a well-adjusted, competent, successful adult. A high instrumental-low expressive combination characterizes a bookworm who is socially invisible and ineffectual but is successful at scholarly activity. A low instrumental-high expressive combination is characteristic of a mediocre student who is socially effective and loyal to the school and what it stands for, both expressively and instrumentally. A low instrumental-low expressive combination characterizes the alienated youth who can find no rewards in the school.

Through a creative use of its expressive culture, the average inner-city school can make itself a place of constructive influence in the lives of its pupils, can teach them some of its values, and can find opportunity to help them achieve higher levels in the instrumental culture.

Practical Examples of Value Teaching

It is a safe assumption that those pupils who do best in knowledge and skill departments of the school are the ones who learn the values of the school most adequately. Consequently, a number of inner-city innovations involve the best half of the class or the school.

The New York City Demonstration—Guidance Project: 1957-62

This project was begun in Junior High School 43, located at the edge of the Harlem slum area of New York City. Ethnically, the pupils were 48 per cent Negro, 38 per cent Puerto Rican, and 14 per cent "others." The ablest half of the total school population of 1,400 were selected for the project. They had a median verbal IQ of 95, and were, on the average, a year and a half retarded both in reading and in mathematics. Placed in smaller classes than usual, and given much more counseling than the other students, they were subject to a number of motivating influences designed to change their values in the direction of greater liking for the school and greater respect and desire for education. They were given a program of cultural enrichment, including trips to theaters, ballets, museums, consulates, and special cinema showings. Their parents were brought into the project through small and large group meetings.

While half of the group were lost to the project through not entering the George Washington Senior High School, those who entered the senior high school graduated in substantially greater numbers than those from the same junior high school in pre-project years. At graduation, 57 pupils from the 258 who graduated from high school were cited for various distinctions, some several times. Of the graduates, 168 went on to a higher institution compared with 47 pupils from the three classes preceding the experiment. It seems clear that there were some important value changes in the experimental group (Hillson and Myers, 1963).

The Kansas City Special Scholarship Program: 1962-66

This is an experimental effort to increase college attendance among students from economically, culturally, and educationally marginal segments of the population. Students are nominated by their teachers for the program while they are in the first or second year of high school. They and their parents are advised that they are college material and that scholarship aid will be given to them if they do well in high school. The mean IQ of the four groups of high school seniors was about 110. They are all from low-income families, and need financial assistance to attend college. A special scholarship fund is available for them.

During the summer following high school graduation, the group attends an eight-week "College Readiness Class." They are informed that, if they do satisfactory work, they will be awarded adequate scholarship help to go to college for four years. Out of 119 in the 1964 group, 13 withdrew from this course, and 29 were graded "unsatisfactory." Some of those marked "unsatisfactory" were evaluated by the staff as follows:

Boy—No work in reading the first half of term. Poor study habits, unorganized, failed to use library time wisely. Lacking in language sense. Bored, very critical of all aspects of the program.

Boy—A wonderful personality. Serious deficiency in language background. Accepts criticism—seeks help. Just too weak to overcome deficiencies in one summer session.

Girl—Playful, slow to get organized. Evades responsibility. Fails to produce, work often incomplete.

Girl—Many class absences. Poor study habits, wastes time. Insolent attitude is a block to learning. Careless with the truth. Absent from final. No term paper in composition.

On the other hand, several hundred students have entered college under this program and about 75 per cent of them will graduate. One student from the successful group is James (Wheeler, 1963).

James is a Negro boy. He was seventeen at the time he was being considered for financial assistance. James had a rather outstanding elementary school record, but his performance in junior high school was spasmodic. His record in senior high school was indifferent. However, at the beginning of the eleventh grade, his work improved. He had taken a program heavy with mathematics and science and had consistently earned good grades in these subjects.

James' parents were divorced. He lived with his mother and stepfather. He had two sisters. Both had married at an early age and had moved away from home.

The school counselor reported that although James verbalized an interest in college enrollment, he did not complete his application for scholarship help. Nevertheless, the counselor continued to see James and later arranged for an interview for him and his parents with the director of scholarships.

By this time, the school counselor had detected evidence of considerable resentment in James' attitude toward his parents, especially his mother.

The parents did not keep their first appointment for interview. The director made several telephone calls, and finally was able to see James' parents. The stepfather did not feel obligated to help with James' enrollment in college in any way. He refused to complete information asked for in the financial statement, and was belligerent throughout the entire session. The mother did not believe that college enrollment was a real possibility for her son. She did not disapprove of the stepfather's attitude, and, more or less, accepted his decision as final.

Other ways were found for assessing family income. James continued to claim an interest in college enrollment. He was awarded a full scholarship to one of the state universities, which he accepted. James attended the College Readiness Class for the first part of the summer at the expense of the scholarship program. He found a job afterward. During the middle of August, he contacted the director, and said that he would not enroll in college in September. He planned to continue on his job.

After several interviews with James, he decided to give college a try. He appeared at a general meeting of scholarship recipients with his mother. A few weeks later, he left for college.

At the end of the first semester, during a visit to James on the college campus, it was learned that he had been named to the Dean's list for high academic performance. His grades in science and mathematics were consistently high. He was enthusiastic about his college career. His teachers were very complimentary regarding his diligence and performance in the classroom. James was employed as an assistant in the physics laboratory.

Conclusions

Knowledge, skills, and values are interrelated and the teacher of an inner-city school has a problem of closing the gap between her and the pupils in all three areas. The value gap is more perplexing than the knowledge and skills gaps because the teacher cannot teach values as directly as she can knowledge and skills, and there may be some disagreement between the teacher and parents of pupils on the important values. But this disagreement may easily be magnified by teachers who are unsure of themselves and of the program in which they are working.

The inner-city school can work to help the pupil acquire a set of values which tend to make him competent in an urban, industrial, and democratic society. These values are not in conflict with the value systems of the working class. The problem of the teacher is not to overcome a hostile set of values, but to help pupils whose values are confused and underdeveloped to clarify their values and to work effectively toward the realization of them.

E. Paul Torrance

Fostering Creative Behavior

There are many quite legitimate reasons why all teachers should be interested in fostering creative behavior among their pupils. All of us would like to see our pupils achieve their potentialities and learn as much as they are capable of learning. However, children cannot do this if they are taught in such a way that their creative thinking abilities have little or no chance of being used in the quest for knowledge. It also seems clear that creative growth is necessary for mental health, a fully-functioning personality, educational achievement, later vocational success, and useful social contributions (Torrance, 1962, 1965a).

I know some inner-city teachers who value highly the creative potential of their pupils, foster such behavior, and help their classes achieve new heights of human dignity. However, two opposing attitudes are embraced by other inner-city teachers with whom I have spoken. Some of them believe that discipline is such a serious problem that fostering creative behavior would cause them to lose control of their classes and that destructiveness and chaos would result. They fear that the release of creativity would unloose primitive impulses that would be overwhelming to them and their pupils. Others perceive their pupils as apathetic and listless and maintain that it is impossible to foster creative behavior among them. Perhaps there are some very real reasons why one group of teachers fears creative behavior and the other is unable to foster it. It is my hope that in this discussion I can help both groups of teachers better understand the forces that inhibit creative behavior and the means of guiding it to constructive achievement.

Environmental Forces That Inhibit Creative Behavior

Success-Orientation

It is frequently alleged that we have in the United States the most success-oriented culture in the world. We are reminded that both our military and civilian educational systems prepare individuals only for success, not for coping with frustration and failure. Everything must be prevented. Evidence of the inhibiting effects of this orientation emerges repeatedly in the testing of children with creative thinking tasks. For example, many children refuse to think of the things that Mother Hubbard could have done when she found the cupboard bare. It just never should have happened!

This success-orientation is inimical to creative behavior, because creative ways of learning involve experimentation, taking risks, making mistakes, and correcting them. If making mistakes is forbidden and results in severe punishment, children soon give up all hopes of succeeding and cease their efforts to learn and grow. As a result, some of them become apathetic and refuse to be stimulated and others resort to aggressiveness, hostility, and destructiveness. To foster constructive creative behavior, the inner-city teacher may have to modify his concept of success in the classroom to permit children to succeed first in ways that are possible for them and use the resulting growth to guide them to higher levels of creative behavior. Think of the predicament of the teacher who described the following experience with a group of low achieving (unsuccessful) boys:[1]

---

[1] The incidents quoted in this discussion were contributed by students enrolled in my class, "Creative Ways of Teaching," and are used with their permission.

Several years ago, in a seventh and eighth grade school, we had a period at the end of the day for special interests. I offered to lead a science club. . . . I had a well-equipped science room and a good science background. I was a little taken back when my group turned out to be fifteen of the lowest achieving boys in the school, but we set to work in the lab.

We had a good time! The custodian did not approve. . . . The boys spent all summer working on a project, perfected it in the science interest class the next year, entered it in the San Francisco Science Fair, and won a prize. These boys had only average I.Q.'s, came from problem homes, and were not *students*. . . . I have always been proud of these boys.

What would have been the most likely outcome if this teacher had not modified his success-orientation, at least for a while?

Children who have established patterns of failure may succeed even at difficult tasks, when motivated and given a chance to succeed. Maurice, as described by one of his teachers, was such a child:

Maurice was a large, passionate-eyed, blond who had been retained in third grade because he couldn't read and was thought to be "dull-minded." His interest seemed to be in science and in working with his delicate, sensitive hands. The class decided to make a dinosaur out of papier-mâché, so we made a table-sized brontosaurus, then a somewhat larger stegosaurus. Maurice didn't become very involved in either of these two projects. One day he said, "These dinosaurs are pretty good, but if I made one it would be the tyrannosaurus [king]." It then occurred to me that this boy wanted and needed to be leader, so I permitted this production. He worked on it for weeks. (I fought guilt feelings because now he was so absorbed that he didn't want to read at all, but he was involved, really involved, in this tyrannosaurus.) It was a big success—it was so big— 8 feet tall, about 2 feet wide. He donated it to my future third graders. Shortly after this, I felt a growing confidence within this boy. His reading progress was a miracle. He lost his fear—and it was a fear that he would never read like the others. Maurice reads far above grade level and does a variety of interesting things.

It is natural for teachers to discourage children who habitually fail in ordinary tasks from undertaking extraordinary tasks for fear that they will only continue to fail. Such children may be challenged, however, by extraordinary tasks and rise to the occasion through all-out creative efforts. They may then be able to establish patterns of success.

Peer-Orientation

Anthropologists tell us that we have the most peer-oriented culture on earth. Evidence of the inhibiting effects of peer pressures to conformity on creative thinking is too obvious to enumerate. Such evidence appears when we observe children and young people, when we conduct sociometric studies, and when we study the creative writings of youngsters. It is quite likely that these phenomena are responsible, in a large part, for the sharp drop in the curves of creative development that occurs in the fourth and seventh grades. About the time a child reaches the fourth grade, his need for consensual validation of his ideas is intensified. He becomes afraid to think until he learns what his peers are thinking. Unusual or original ideas are common targets of peer pressures to conformity or uniformity.

That these pressures operate in the inner city is evidenced by the responses of forty-five seventh graders selected by the faculty of an inner-city school as likely dropouts. Ninety-five per cent of them said that they did not think their ideas and suggestions would be taken seriously by the rest of the class. Seventy-three per cent indicated that they were afraid their ideas and suggestions would be laughed at by their classmates. An equal number also indicated that even though others might not laugh at their ideas, their classmates would still not like their ideas. Seventy per cent of them indicated that they believe the best answer is the one the class decides is right. It would appear that they have no chance of obtaining approval for their ideas and have as a consequence stopped responding creatively to problems. Such children frequently appear estranged and out of contact with reality. They may seem apathetic and become classified as mentally retarded. Such was the case of Jamie as revealed in the following incident described by his fifth-grade teacher:

Jamie lived on another planet. He seemed to feel no need to relate to the world around him. As he entered the fifth grade, the children thought of him as a "dumb kid." In a flexible, individualized reading program, I was able to let him skip around in the book as the spirit moved him and report in the way he was able, through drawings. He completed one fourth-grade and two fifth-grade readers during the year, and I feel he is ready to face any sixth-grade material.

At the same time, in a "slow" math class he was exposed to an imaginative teacher. By allowing him to use his interest in motors to develop a math project, he was able to show a real flair for teaching others, and his classmates discovered that Jamie had brains!

Thus, we have another example of how an inner-city teacher encouraged a child to behave creatively and used the gains therefrom to help him attain peer acceptance.

There are times when it is even possible to use a child's creative contribution to enlist the cooperation of an entire class in helping him succeed. The following incident is an example of how this was accomplished in one fourth-grade class:

When Dana entered my fourth-grade class, the principal gave me a bulging cumulative folder with much information about Dana's previous undesirable behavior and non-learning experiences. He had been retained in the third grade and had run away from school on frequent occasions. He had a severe speech problem and stuttered so badly that he was most difficult to understand.

It was difficult at the beginning because the children didn't accept him and they were tempted to mimic him. I decided not to push the reading skills and let Dana enter the discussion group in reading of his own choice. (He later asked to read and take part in a puppet show.) I talked the principal out of any extra help except for the speech therapist who was a kind man and provided a good male relationship for Dana.

I discovered Dana had talent in art through a hand puppet show. He became the art director for the reading group and this later developed into the position of art consultant for the classroom. Dana's self-respect and prestige blossomed. He created many new ideas for the class. He never missed a day of school and worked diligently in every subject.

But the greatest half-hour in every student's life that fall was when Dana enthusiastically, but respectfully, read (stuttered) his two-page report on snakes while the whole class listened respectfully and quietly. It was really a thrill for everyone in the classroom because we all felt a part of Dana's great achievement. We had all learned so much.

Dana moved a month later and he was expelled from the new school for being a behavior problem.

Dana's story illustrates how a teacher's ability to become aware of a child's creative potential and to use it for the good of the group can influence the peer culture to support and foster healthy development. It also illustrates the tragedy of lost talent when this is not done.

Sanctions Against Questioning and Exploration

Although teachers generally recognize the need for children to ask questions and in other ways inquire about the wonders and mysteries around them, such tendencies are frequently squelched. Forty-three per cent of the seventh graders identified as potential dropouts in an inner-city school indicated that they were afraid to ask questions in class. This statistic becomes especially meaningful when compared with the finding that only seventeen per cent of a sample of fourth graders indicated that they were afraid to ask questions (Torrance and Gupta, 1964a). The child who is afraid to ask questions is likely to become closed to new experiences and new information. Such a child is truly a culturally disadvantaged child.

Teachers never find it easy to be patient with the child who is always asking searching questions and exploring the world about him. They ask such embarrassing questions as, "Mr. Olson, would you turn Communist if the Russians captured the United States?" "Why do you need two rabbits to have little rabbits?" They become so absorbed in something they are exploring that it is almost impossible to pull away from it so that the class can move forward to a new activity. According to inner-city school teachers many so-called culturally disadvantaged children are notorious for becoming so absorbed in an object or problem that their attention cannot be diverted to new interests. Even preschool children show this kind of creative behavior, as illustrated by the following incident:

A three-year-old, on a walk with the class, was shown a snail. Completely fascinated, he spent the remaining school time (one and one-half hours) observing and touching the snail, but I let him alone while the rest of us went on with crafts. The child consequently became so interested in nature's small creatures that at age five he is quite an authority on them.

Misplaced Emphasis on Sex Roles

Both boys and girls suffer in their creative development as a result of society's overemphasis or misplaced emphasis on sex roles. Both simply shut out certain areas of awareness. Creative behavior, by its very nature, requires sensitivity and independence of thinking. In our culture, sensitivity and receptiveness are definitely feminine virtues while independence in thinking is considered a masculine attribute. Thus, highly creative boys are likely to appear more effeminate than their peers and highly creative girls, more masculine than theirs.

The crippling effects of these misplaced emphases on sex differences are likely to be most acute among inner-city children. Boys in particular are taught to guard fiercely their masculinity from an early age. This may include being taught rather harshly that talkativeness is girlish and not to be tolerated in little boys. In the school that values highly verbal skills this places boys at a great disadvantage. Sex differences appear to be especially marked in the inner-city school. For example, among the potential dropouts in seventh and eighth grades of one school, I found that about 90 per cent of the girls and only about 15 per cent of the boys indicated that "the best answer should be the one that the teacher thinks is right." Thus, it appears that the potential female dropout in the inner-city school may have been trained to be over-receptive to the authority of the teacher while the boy may have been trained to be over-rejecting of such authority.

Divergency Equated with Abnormality

Once even leading scholars believed "genius" and "madness" to be associated with one another. Almost all inventors, composers, creative scientists, and other creative persons were regarded as insane. Although these beliefs were discredited long ago, somehow the belief has persisted that any divergence from behavioral norms is an indication of something abnormal, unhealthy, or immoral and to be corrected at all costs.

Rather than cultivate the model of the so-called normal, well-rounded person, the inner-city teacher in many cases would perhaps be wise to cultivate the idiosyncrasies and peculiar strengths of a particular child. Frank Riessman (1965a), for example, has suggested that teachers of culturally deprived children build upon the common strengths of such children rather than expend energies in helping them overcome handicaps or defects in their backgrounds. To cite an example, he maintains that the culturally disadvantaged child may be slow but not dull and may suffer when speed is at a premium. Riessman suggests there are virtues in slowness, however, and programs can be built upon them. He also offers positive proposals for action on the culturally deprived child's hidden verbal ability and his positive attitude toward education. Riessman sees the lack of "know how" as the culturally deprived child's basic weakness—how to fill out forms, to take tests, to answer questions, to listen, and to appear for interviews. He also feels that the culturally deprived child's anti-intellectual attitude is a handicap and should be modified.

At times the inner-city teacher may have to look to behavior not approved by the school for signs of creative potential. It may not occur in the kinds of behavior valued by the school, at least not until it is recognized in the disapproved behavior and given intelligent guidance and direction. The following rather dramatic incident described by a sixth-grade teacher in an inner-city school shows that this is possible:

> The principal, the janitor, the teachers all worked on the problem of John, the vandal. He was reported as being the culprit of many a weekend shambles at our school, but no one could prove anything. He couldn't stay still very long; his iron muscles seemed to need to move every minute; he was as strong at twelve years as most grown men. He was almost a permanent fixture in the office because of undesirable behavior. He was skilled, a *natural*, in things mechanical. He liked to boss and was often swaggering and bully-like in his playground behavior. The consensus, as a result of brainstorming, was that John did not feel he belonged. The problem was how to make him feel he *did* belong.
>
> He was appointed by the Student Council (in which he could never be an officer because of their strict code of grades and behav-

ior) to be a chairman of the Lunchroom Committee. He organized a team of boys, helping the janitor. He began to notice the litter which collected in certain windy corners of the schoolyard. His "gang" cleaned it up. He helped park cars for Back-to-School Night. . . . He had organized the entire parking area without a hitch, where the drivers followed his directions, and all this done as well as an adult could have done it.

Happily, as John became "part" of the school, the vandalism became less and less. Reports came to us that he threatened (and coming from this boy that was no mean threat) others who tried to destroy school property. Happily, he began to take an interest in schoolwork. His father told us that John had at last said "I like school." He said that John had learned to read things around the house, in the neighborhood, at the store, and on trips for the first time in his life. His art work (racing cars, car engines, and antique cars) was excellent. We all hope some of this progress will continue when he leaves us this fall to go to junior high school.

What Teachers Can Do To Meliorate Inhibiting Forces

Along with the identification and description of some of the environmental forces that inhibit creative behavior, I have tried to show through data supplied me by experienced teachers that it is possible for teachers in inner-city schools to meliorate these inhibiting forces and foster constructive creative behavior. Now, I shall attempt to sketch, in a somewhat systematic way, some of the kinds of things that I believe teachers in inner-city schools can do to foster creative behavior and reduce the inhibiting influences of the environmental forces discussed in the preceding section. I shall suggest ideas that may be practiced by individual teachers as well as by groups of teachers in a school.[2]

Being Respectful of Questions and Ideas

I believe that almost every teacher could immediately begin to increase the learning and creative functioning of his pupils by sincerely respecting their questions and ideas. One of the first require-

---

[2] Many of these ideas were originally developed in a series of ten articles in *The Instructor*, 1964-65.

ments for creative behavior is the capacity to wonder, to be puzzled, and to respond constructively. Children have this capacity and their curiosity impels them to ask questions and to seek answers, usually with great energy and enthusiasm. This questioning, however, is frequently inconvenient, irritating, threatening, and generally up-setting to adults.

Being respectful of children's questions is not easy for teachers. It requires that the teacher respond with interest and curiosity rather than with threats and punishment. Poor questions must be seen as an opportunity to teach the class how to ask good questions. It re-quires helping children to find answers to questions and making the effort worthwhile. In fact, the most important reward to the curious child is finding answers to his questions. The teacher does not have to answer the questions of children immediately, and in some cases need not answer questions at all. The creative teacher knows how to enrich the period between the question and the answer. He seldom gives answers that can be discovered by the pupils them-selves. He leads them to produce, consider, and evaluate a wide range of possibilities.

Children should be taught to test their ideas, but this testing has to be done in a sympathetic and constructive atmosphere rather than a hostile and punitive one. The teacher who respects children's ideas avoids making fun of the ideas presented, the songs and poems com-posed, and the conclusions reached by children. Such a teacher shows children how to test ideas for reasonableness against what they already know and tries to establish habits and attitudes that make such testing commonplace.

To develop these skills I propose that teachers as individuals or in workshop groups try the following:

1. Think about what it really means to be respectful of the questions and ideas of children.
2. Try deliberately to be respectful of the questions and ideas of their pupils.
3. Write detailed descriptions of one incident in which they tried to be respectful of an unusually vexing question and one incident in which they tried to be respectful of an original idea presented by a pupil.
4. Discuss their descriptions with one another, trying to decide how

well the teacher succeeded in being respectful of the pupil's questions and ideas—not just appearing to be respectful. It is suggested that the group then try to produce a variety of other possible ways by which the teacher could have been more respectful.

As one of the first steps, I suggest that teachers write out descriptions of incidents in which they tried to apply this principle. The following set of questions might be used as a guide:

1. What was the question (idea)? Who asked (expressed) it? What were the general conditions under which it was asked (proposed)?

2. What was your own immediate reaction?

3. What was the immediate reaction of the class?

4. In what way was respect shown for the question (idea)?

5. What, if any, were the observable effects (immediate and/or long range)?

In workshops, the success of this procedure will depend upon the degree to which the members feel comfortable and unthreatened and are willing to expose their values and behavior patterns so that perceptions and reactions can be changed. I firmly believe that almost every teacher could improve learning immediately by asking more provocative questions. By doing this, teachers would also increase excitement about learning, acquisition of information, ability to recall information in problem solving, and depth of understanding.

In a recent article for elementary teachers (Torrance, 1964b), I pointed out that some surveys indicate over 90 per cent of the questions teachers ask call only for the reproduction of what is in the textbook. One of the "Letters to the Editor" published later was by a teacher who said that she could "go me one better," that 100 per cent of her questions called only for the recall of what is in the textbook. She wrote that in her opinion the first job of the teacher is to decide what students ought to know and that the second is to make sure that they learn it. I think she misunderstood what I was trying to say. I was not saying that there are not some things that are important enough to memorize. The main thing that I was trying to say is that it is important for pupils to think about what they learn and do something with what they learn.

In a workshop which purports to improve the ability of teachers to ask provocative questions, something must be done to help instructors see what some of the different kinds of questions are, other than factual. A number of conceptual schemes may be used for this purpose. One well-known scheme (Bloom, 1956) uses such categories as knowledge, comprehension, application, analysis, synthesis, and evaluation. Perhaps a project might involve the deliberate attempt to think of questions that fall into each of these categories—that is, questions requiring:

1. *depth of comprehension*—the translation of what is learned from one level of abstraction to another, the interpretation of what is learned, and extrapolation or going beyond the information to determine implications, consequences, and effects.

2. *application of information*—showing how they will use the information if given a situation in which no method of solution is specified.

3. *analysis*—involving identification and classification of the elements in a problem, the showing of relationships, and the discovery of organizational principles involved.

4. *synthesis*—the recombining of previously learned information with new information into original and useful ideas.

5. *evaluation*—the showing of awareness of problems, deficiencies, and gaps in information.

Since many children have been so thoroughly accustomed to the idea that each question asked in school has a single correct answer, it is important for teachers to develop the skills of asking questions that call for divergent thinking. By this, I mean questions that would call for:

1. *fluency*—the production of as many ideas as possible, not bothering at first about quality.

2. *flexibility*—shifting to a variety of approaches.

3. *originality*—unusual or uncommon ideas, away from the obvious.

4. *elaboration*—working out the details of an idea, planning the steps, etc.

In some of my own workshops, I ask participants to think of as many provocative questions as they can about *ice*. I try to communicate to them what I mean by provocative questions, using *apple* as an example. I tell them that I am not interested in simple factual questions such as "What colors do apples come in?" "How many seeds do apples have?" and the like. I want them to ask provocative questions such as "What was there about the apple that caused God to use it to tempt Eve rather than some other fruit?" After this, I give them a list of questions about ice and ask them to pick out the five questions that they consider most provocative. Following these two exercises, we score both the questions they produced and the questions they selected using Burkhart and Bernheim's (1963) criteria for evaluating unusual questions. They recognize, then, that many of the questions they asked are purely factual, are not self-involving, and do not call for thinking, especially divergent thinking. They also begin to sense what I mean by the provocativeness of a question and the potential that this has for producing deep learning.

Recognizing and Valuing Originality

I believe that all teachers should be on the lookout for original ideas and place as much value on them as on the acquisition of information. Of course, there is no point in originality or divergency for itself. Thus, teachers will want to place requirements other than rarity, remoteness, or divergence from the obvious and commonplace on the kind of originality that they encourage. Some teachers look for responses that are true, generalizable, and surprising in the light of what the student knew at the time he produced the idea or made the discovery.

To develop the skills of recognizing and valuing originality, a teacher should deliberately try, for a given period, to recognize and encourage original responses in pupils. Since the love for the one correct response is usually so firmly established, the help of supervisors or fellow teachers in a workshop is useful. One way is to write out detailed descriptions of some of these attempts and analyze them or get someone else to do so. In writing these descriptions, the following questions are suggested as guides:

1. In what form did original ideas by the child occur?
2. What was the immediate reaction of the teacher?
3. What were the reactions of the other children?

4. How was respect shown for the original idea?

5. What were the immediate effects of respecting the original idea?

6. What were the long-range effects?

Developing Ability to Elaborate

Teachers always feel pressed for time because there is so much material to cover. In my opinion, they would accomplish much more if they would help their pupils uncover and discover just a few things by giving them opportunities for elaboration. Original thinkers need to elaborate their ideas if they are to become meaningful and useful.

Even people who are not very original can make important contributions by elaborating an idea produced by someone else or even a commonplace idea. Some people have a low regard for this kind of creativity, but our society needs people who can work out the details of ideas and make ideas practical and attractive. We sometimes call them "embroiderers" because they make ideas "fancy." Of course, a person can be too "fancy" and his work loses its real meaning and worth. Yet a certain level of ability to elaborate seems necessary for adequate adjustment. In one study (Will, 1964), it was found that the most characteristic feature of the thinking of a group of delinquent girls was their inability to elaborate. On the other hand, in a group of home economists in the Peace Corps, all of whom were unusually high on elaboration ability, this ability was negatively related to effectiveness as a Peace Corps worker (Hanson, 1964). What happened here was that all of them were adequate elaborators, but some of them became so lost in their elaboration and made things so fancy that it interfered with their effectiveness in underdeveloped countries.

In the classroom, teachers might want to focus on encouraging elaboration in reading stories. Some reading experts believe that well-developed exercises in elaborative thinking in reading will produce higher permanent retention and greater availability of information to new situations. One of the most common methods of elaborating what is read is to have children illustrate the poems and stories that they read. Other media, such as music, songs, rhythmic movement, and dramatics can also be used in elaborating what is read. Having pupils write different endings for stories, change a character in some specific way and see what else this would change, and expand upon a certain episode in a story or poem are other ideas for elaborating what is read.

Teachers might select a child who is unusually unresponsive and give him experiences in elaborating what he hears or reads by his favorite media. This precedure has been known to "unlock" some students having this difficulty and to serve as the key to their learning.

Developing Creative Readers

It is easier to remember and to use something read creatively than things read passively or even critically. When a child reads creatively, he is sensitive to problems and possibilities. To resolve this tension, he sees new relationships and possibilities, synthesizes unrelated elements, redefines or transforms known information into new uses, and builds onto what he already knows. Thus, he produces multiple possibilities, looks at information in greater depth, and fills in gaps to make ideas useful, attractive, and exciting.

It takes effort, however, to change from a passive or critical reader into a creative one. Teachers can help children become creative readers in two major ways: heightening their expectations and anticipations and encouraging them to do something with what they read. I have discussed these two approaches in some detail in *Gifted Children in the Classroom* (1965c).

Heightening expectation involves some creation of tension or warming up. Doing something with what is read can occur at any one of four different levels:

1. Reproducing with imagination what is read, making things sound like the thing happening.
2. Elaborating what is read, as already discussed.
3. Transforming and rearranging what is read, as illustrated by Shakespeare's creativity.
4. Going beyond what is read.

In a workshop for educators, I would suggest that the first week be spent in helping the teacher become a more creative reader. The teacher should practice heightening his own expectations and anticipation when he reads; try guessing what a story or book will be like, what its characters will be like, and experiences they will have. It is suggested that he stop at some point and try to predict the outcomes, and that he try to do something with what he has read. He should try to read or tell stories with imagination, making them sound like the thing happening; elaborate what he reads, transform or rearrange something read; and let his imagination take him beyond what he reads. It is anticipated that teachers who imaginatively apply these ideas to their own reading will become so enthusiastic that they will be unable to wait until the second week to begin teaching their pupils to become more creative readers.

Searching for the Truth with Methods of Research

Since the very essence of genuine learning as well as creativity is "searching for the truth," attention should be given to the development of the skills of searching for the truth. Without these skills, children will lack genuine depth in their learning and thinking. Teachers should recognize that no subject—not even history—is a body of precise, memorizable facts. Historical interpretations change when we examine events at different times and places. An idea or event may be ignored at the time it occurred but take on much significance at a different time. Children should cultivate the habit of re-evaluating information and considering alternative possibilities concerning causes and consequences. This calls for the skills and spirit of historiography.

Teachers should be familiar with the thinking processes and methods involved in historiography and given examples of how these methods can be applied to different subjects at all grade levels. Even children in the primary grades can study the changes that have taken place on their block during their lives or in their school building since they entered school. Children in the intermediate grades can use primary sources to try to determine which of several pictures of Christopher Columbus or of the Battle of Lexington tells the truth. In a short course on research methods, I teach sixth graders some of the skills of historiography through constructing from various witnesses and records their own growth curves from kindergarten through sixth grade with such things as height, weight, reading speed, vocabulary size, and curiosity. They immediately become involved in such problems as units of measurement, bias, conflicting information, inaccurate information, and the critical and creative processes of synthesizing information and getting at the truth. I have described these and other methods in *Rewarding Creative Behavior: Experiments in Classroom Creativity* (1965b).

As a workshop experience, I suggest that each teacher create and test at least one lesson through which they deliberately attempt to develop some of the skills of historiography. Such a lesson might be about what happened in school or at home yesterday, the changes in the school building during the last year, or an event in American or world history. It should involve the collection, evaluation, and synthesis of several kinds of information.

Methods of descriptive research enable us to tell more accurately and truthfully what *is*. Historiography helps us tell more truthfully what *was*, and experimental methods permit us to predict what *will be* if certain factors are carefully controlled. Methods of descriptive research capture the results of experiments conducted by nature and society, while historiography helps discover the results of experiments conducted by time. A third method, experimental research, determines the effect of possible changes, procedures, and kinds of organization.

Focus in descriptive research is on existing conditions, or on how a person, group, or thing behaves in the present. It often involves comparisons or contrasts, such as differences between the behavior of boys and girls or second graders and third graders. For use in the workshop on methods of descriptive research, I have suggested five visual aids from a little book, created by Karl G. Anderson of Berkeley, in my class, "Creative Ways of Teaching." The book is entitled *Creativity Is* (1964), and is modeled after *Happiness Is* and *Security Is*. Five of the ideas that I feel capture the spirit of descriptive research are:

1. Wanting to know.
2. Looking twice.
3. Listening for smells.
4. Digging deeper.
5. Cutting holes to see through.

These five ideas can be applied in searching for the truth about almost anything. For example, select some object in the room, some event in history, some place in geography, some creative writing assignment. The teacher can then inquire: What do we want to know in order to describe it accurately and truthfully? What can we find out by looking twice? How do we look twice? What do we do in listening for smells (using all of our being)? How can we dig deeper? How can we cut holes to see through (to keep from being deceived, to bring out something that is hidden)?

Children as early as the fifth and sixth grades can generate or collect quantitative data and apply many of the concepts of descriptive statistics, such as the mean, median, mode, range, and variability. Primary children can master simple methods of quantification and graphical representation as ways of describing something. They can construct models, illustrate, photograph, and develop other ways of comparing objects, events, and performances. The important thing, I believe, is to develop the skills for finding out what they want to know, how to look twice, how to listen for smells, how to dig deeper, and how to cut holes to avoid being deceived.

The workshop on searching for the truth with the methods of experimental research should involve participants in some kind of experiment. Special attention should be given to controlling as many variables as possible, the use of randomization, and careful delineation of the experimental conditions or treatments. There are a number of such experiments that are so simple that children in the fifth and sixth grades can conduct them in the lower grades. I have described a number of these in *Gifted Children in the Classroom* (1965c). If possible, the experiments should be designed to find out something that teachers or their pupils want to find out. The experiments should be kept simple enough so that almost immediate results can be obtained and communicated through graphs, simple statistical tests, or the like.

Conclusion

Although these are extremely brief descriptions of creativity workshops for teachers, I have tried to put into them the best that we know from research and theory about the classroom conditions for creative growth. As individual teachers or groups of teachers experiment with my suggestions, they are sure to improve them and other emphases will force themselves to the forefront.

Paul H. Bowman

Improving the Pupil Self-Concept

A few years ago this writer had the opportunity of visiting in a number of schools located in the slum sections of a large South American city. The first impression of a visitor looking at the children in the school was one of overwhelming hopelessness. Most children were barefoot, most were dressed in rags of clothing, and many were afflicted with obvious forms of physical disease. School officials indicated that more than half of the elementary students were in special classes for the mentally retarded. Later visitation to some of the streets and homes in the neighborhood only strengthened the impression that it would require something of a miracle to bring these children to any educational advancement.

As this chapter is being written, many teachers and school administrators in the United States will most likely be having similar experiences in the newly developed "head-start" programs. It is likely that large numbers of children will be discovered who have many dental caries, have never had a medical examination or treatment, who are hungry, who have nutritional deficiencies, who live in intolerable circumstances, who seem to be mentally retarded, and who have a continually disrupted family life. The task of providing such children with a base for a satisfying future life seems insurmountable, since it involves medical and dental care, rehabilitation of housing, employment, and stabilization of families, as well as revitalization of educational experiences.

In the face of such deficiencies it would seem that attention to the self-concept of these pupils might be of low priority, and would scarcely deserve a chapter in this book. Thus, the first question to be discussed in the ensuing paragraphs is the importance of the self-concept in what people do. Secondly, what do children of the inner city think of themselves? And what, if anything, can be done by the teacher in her classroom to bring about positive change in the way her pupils think of themselves?

The Role of the Self-Concept

The modern study of man has developed from the ruminations of philosophers of recent centuries, who, like Bergson, were greatly concerned about "the self." Following the philosophers came the social science theorists who attempted to deal more analytically and systematically with ideas about the self. G. H. Mead talked about the "I" and the "me" (1937), Erikson of identity formation (1960), and Freud of the ego and superego. William James, Henry Stack Sullivan (1953), Karen Horney, Carl Rogers, and others have been centrally concerned with the self-concept in one term or another. In recent years clinicians have been collecting much descriptive data about the functioning of the idea of self in the dynamics of how people behave, and particularly about the role of the self-concept in the changes that take place in people during the process of psychological treatment. Some attempts have been made to quantify and experiment in this area, but only a beginning has been made.

Nonetheless, some working definitions and assumptions have been made upon which many people are proceeding to act, as well as to initiate further studies. The self-concept is described by Jersild as a "composite of thoughts and feelings which constitute a person's awareness of his individual existence, his conception of who and what he is" (Jersild, 1960). It is generally assumed that the way a person thinks of himself determines the general intent and direction of a person's behavior. In other words, persons who think negatively of themselves will behave in self-defeating ways, even though they may choose a variety of behavior patterns in the process. Clinicians have noticed that changes in the way a person conceives of himself are likely to precede outward behavioral changes, and they therefore assume a causative relationship. Some writers think that the shortest route to more accurate prediction of man's behavior, the goal of the science of psychology, is through greater study of the self-concept. They think that there is a historical, scientific base for assuming the self-concept to be very important to any significant change in human behavior.

The importance of self-concept in the education of children is just beginning to be recognized, and its importance to the education of children from the slums is even greater because there is a larger proportion of seriously damaged self-concepts among them. If we are willing to take the time and interest and if we are willing to spend the money, we in this culture know how to clothe the body, to remedy most diseases, to fill teeth and stomachs, and to rehabilitate housing. If we could for a moment assume that all of these things were done for children who needed them, would it follow that they would be well on their way to a more satisfying life? Undoubtedly this is not so. All too often we have complained that tax money has been poured out to provide public housing in former slums, but that ways of living have not changed in any real sense. One of the current assumptions is that many of our welfare programs have failed because they were too piecemeal, that some families may have been provided decent housing but still had empty stomachs, and others may have enjoyed adequate food but were ridden with disease. The programs of the anti-poverty campaign are based on the idea that comprehensive services to families are necessary to rehabilitation, and with this there can be little or no argument. Intensive and comprehensive forms of assistance are necessary conditions to making possible a more productive life for the poor of the nation, but unless these outward changes are accompanied by changed attitudes, motivations, and behaviors, rehabilitation is not likely to "take."

What, then, is the key to helping people in the inner city find more permanent satisfactions, more productive attitudes and behaviors?

Self-Concepts of Inner-City Children

Various estimates have been made by different writers on the number of children that might fall into the category of underprivileged, culturally deprived, or disadvantaged youth. Such estimates vary between 20 and 35 per cent. Whatever it may be, it is quite clear that most of our public schools simply are not providing a very useful or appropriate educational experience for this segment of the school population. Educationally, we are short-changing a large segment of our youth.

However, it is an often forgotten fact that about half of the disadvantaged group still manage to achieve some kind of relative success in school, graduate from high school, and find a relatively satisfactory niche for themselves as adults. At the same time, the other half includes more than its share of school failures, dropouts, delinquents, and adult failures. What are the major differences in these two groups of young people, the successful half of the lowest third and the unsuccessful?

Answers to this question are beginning to come from several different types of investigation, but at present it is still largely speculation. Studies of school dropouts are pointing out that those who leave school are dominated by feelings of defeat, hopelessness, and alienation from peers and adults. The dropout tells us that his parents did not care if he left school or not, and in some cases they even encouraged his withdrawal; his neighbor, who graduated from high school, says that his parents would have "belted" him if he had dropped out, that they insisted that finishing school was the only way to get ahead. Attitude studies show that the "lost" third hate school and teachers, fear anything academic, hate their peers of better status, and carry a chip against society in general. Mental health studies show that members of this group, whether they are aggressive, hostile, fearful, anxious, or quiet, tend to have a high rate of maladjustment.

In other words, the major difference in these two groups is that the young people have different concepts of themselves and come from families that have different self-concepts and values. What are the ways of thinking about self that seem to be associated with the unsuccessful slum child? The following formulations are an attempt to put together the findings from a number of studies and experiences into a composite picture, which, of course, does not accurately reflect any individual (Bowman and Matthews, 1958; Havighurst, Bowman, *et al.*, 1962). It is done with full awareness that it cannot represent the variety of individual differences, but with the hope that it might be useful. Most of these statements came from high school students, but the child of preschool or early elementary years must have many similar feelings. By junior high school years these youth can and do express these concepts verbally and in behavior.

Self-Concepts of the Unsuccessful Disadvantaged Student

These ideas of self seem to center around four main themes, the first of which is failure.

They feel that they always have been and always will be a failure in everything that they attempt to do. They recall neighborhood fights in which they were usually the losers. They compare themselves unfavorably with other siblings of the family. They failed either to get or to hold a part-time job while they were in school, or if they are dropouts they have had even less success in finding a job. They may have tried out for community or school sports and failed to make the grade.

Their strongest feeling of failure is likely to center around their school experiences, for this is the testing ground in which all children attempt to find a degree of adequacy. These children will discover very early in their school careers that they cannot meet the expectations of teachers. During the first days in kindergarten they have to display ignorance of how to use scissors or crayons or books; they cannot use the right words when they talk and have not had experiences with pets as other children, or visits to other towns, or even to places of interest near them. They begin to fear the disapproval and even ridicule of peers and teachers; they try to avoid participating, and in a short time begin to leave school. Most high school dropouts will describe these experiences quite pointedly, as in the following interview excerpts:

You know how teachers do; they talk about stuff and then ask questions about it. I hate that. I never knew what the answer should be and she would get mad and the kids would laugh. That made me feel bad, and I never did like it.

I felt funny when I was first in school. I knew I was some different than the other kids. Not that I was so different, but I knew I couldn't do the things that they did.

Of course, I never did like school. Ever since I was in kindergarten I hated it. Maybe it's because I had to sit in the cloak room so much of the time. I never really got into trouble until the fifth grade, but from then on I didn't like it and me and my buddies just goofed off.

To me they were teaching things that don't have anything to do with English. Things like Julius Caesar and things like that. I don't see any sense in that. I don't see any point in reading things like John Silver and things like that. It seems to me they don't teach you how to talk right. A person ought to learn to talk, learn how to use the right words in the right place.

Question: Is there anything that you need to know on your job that you would have liked to have learned in school?
Answer: No, I don't think there is. My job doesn't have much to do with things like that.

These children are quite aware that their parents are failures. The kind of job the parent holds, or periods of unemployment, or the welfare check, or the house they live in all speak of failure of the parents. Usually there is very little interaction between parents and children. The parents are overburdened, discouraged, and tired; they are frequently out of the home much of the time and children are left on their own resources. When there is interaction, it is usually limited to accomplishing the necessities of daily routines, and these are seldom satisfying (Bernstein, 1961). Thus, the adult models they have usually typify failure.

A second theme is one of alienation from people, and this is also a very pervasive feeling.

For instance, they are aware not only that their parents are failures, but that they themselves are burdens on the parents and frequently not wanted. This concept may result from inferences on the part of the child, but more often than not the idea will be expressed directly in words or specific actions by the parents. Such knowledge may deal a very devastating, if not fatal, blow to any possibility of positive self-esteem by a youngster. One high school boy brought out the following in a small group discussion:

> I want to get a job and be able to leave home as soon as possible. A boy shouldn't be in his parents' way. They have enough problems with the younger kids. Anyway I know they don't want me around. My mother told me several times—whenever she gets good and mad —that she tried to have me aborted, but it didn't work. That's pretty clear, isn't it?

A feeling of alienation from their own age mates is just as evident, and especially rejection, real or fancied, by their peers of more privileged economic circumstances is constantly talked about.

> Those high-class girls think they are better than anyone else. They got a lot of money. They don't like us and we don't like them. They seem to look down on us kids in this neighborhood; you know, they think we are scabs.

> In class the rich kids always had their lessons. They never came in without their lessons. Then if us kids didn't have ours, and we usually didn't, they would look at us. One time we decided to try to get in with these high-class kids, but we didn't get to the first step. It seems like they have a class of their own and you just can't break in.

> [A boy] They never speak to me and they always wear better clothes than I do. They wear thirty and forty dollar outfits and expect other people to do the same. If you don't, they think you are dirt under their feet. Why, I wouldn't wear suit pants out there. I know those guys have jeans to wear, but they got to show you up by wearing fancy clothes.

These social-class barriers might be expected to drive the rejected lower-class child into closer association with persons of his own status. This, however, does not seem to be the case. The girls, particularly, seem to be lonely and without friends, but even for the boys who form clubs or gangs the actual friendship ties are very weak, if they exist at all. These associations seem to be liaisons for mutual support among the rejected rather than close personal ties.

> [A girl] I didn't have any friends. I didn't associate with kids at

junior high; there was just me and my sister. I just didn't like the kids. I knew them but I didn't run around with anyone.

[A boy] That's a funny thing about me. Anybody who is outspoken and mean, I seem to pick up with them. I don't mind telling people off and other kids see that, and pretty soon they hook up with you. Maybe that's why I don't always get in with the right people . . . The trouble with me is that I like to be in with a group but I just don't know how to mix with kids. I never knew how.

I found that at junior high everybody had their friends. I tried to be friendly and speak to kids but it didn't do much good. I say that a pleasant smile and a greeting never hurt anyone.

Further evidence of alienation is found in participation of these young people in the extracurricular activities of the school, or rather their lack of participation. In one dropout study, it was found that none of these youth had even held a position as an officer in an extracurricular activity, one-fourth of them had never participated in any way in such activities, and of those who did participate, their activity was usually limited to attendance at athletic events and school dances.

I never went to any of the games and dances. Oh, I went to one football game in the eighth grade, but I did not like it and that was enough.
Q: Do you feel that you were generally a part of the junior high school as far as the activities were concerned?
A: No, I don't. I went to one dance and stayed for ten minutes. I never went to another one.
Q: Do you feel like you were happy in junior high?
A: Just before school started and after school was out.

The neighbors of these dropouts who stayed in school were often involved in some specific activity, such as band, an athletic team, or a club.

A third theme of thinking about the self of the unsuccessful student is that of seeing himself usually as a victim in many of his life situations, of feeling that other people are out to take him whenever they can, of feeling that he seldom gets the fair chance that he deserves. This seems to be the major criterion in their judgment of teachers; that is, whether teachers are fair or not in their dealings. The teachers they liked and respected were described in these terms: "They didn't jump on me if I did anything wrong," "They didn't think I was any better or worse than the next guy." The teachers they didn't like were described as follows:

> He always jumped on me when I didn't do anything except sit there and laugh at the boys.
>
> Something was done in the class and I was blamed for it. I guess they figured that because I had done some things before, I had done this too.
>
> She was constantly on me. I either had a pencil in my hand, or I was chewing my nails, or there was always something wrong with me.
>
> She wouldn't let me make up work when I was absent or anything like that, but she let other kids.
>
> She didn't like the way I did my work and criticized me in front of the class. I always say a teacher can bawl you out in private, but . . .

Probably 90 per cent of the criticisms of teachers center around mistreatment of students. They feel that they have been victimized, and many of the incidents were based on fact, although some apparently were not.

These three themes of self appraisal all too frequently lead to a fourth; namely, that of hopelessness, of feeling that there is nothing in the future worth preparing for. These expressions of aimlessness, lack of purpose or goal, are found at many age levels.

> I couldn't get along with teachers; that is the main reason I quit. I really didn't like any of them. In a way it seems better being out of school and in a way it don't. When you are in school, at least you have some place to go and pass the time.

> I do wish I could have graduated from high school. I'd give a million for that. It makes you feel that you are something. People ask you what you have done. I really haven't done anything, but I would be somebody anyway if I finished high school. When I got kicked out I just sat down in the hall and cried.

> [A composition] When I was a boy in fust grade I was slow in most everthing I did. I usual had to stay after school and finish my work. That was first time I flunk. The second and threeth grads went by

and I didn't learn anything. Fourth grade I was flunk again. What was my trouble? I never couldn't learn to reade and no one saw to it that I did. I am seventeen and in the tenth grade and I still don't know how to read good. And when you can't read you soon get discouraged. And when I use your sentence "Finally I gave up the search in despair" I am talking of hope of learning to read. [A boy with IQ of 120]

These, then, seem to be the main themes in the way most disadvantaged children think of themselves—failure, stupidity, alienation from others, unfairness in their personal dealings by others, and hopelessness.

The Educational Problem

Let us shift our attention now to the elementary school in an inner-city neighborhood and define the educational task that confronts the school staff if they are to be successful in bringing meaningful educational experiences to these children. I suppose it would be agreed that little learning will take place if children are hungry, cold, or ill. The only hurdle in meeting such needs is the will of the community to provide the necessary resources; the knowledge and the trained personnel exist in practically every community. This is usually regarded as the function of the welfare or public health programs, but in some parts of the world this function has to be discharged by the school itself, with medical, dental, nursing, and feeding services in every elementary school. In this country the school can no longer assume that this task will be performed by someone else. It must assure itself that physical needs are being met, or initiate some action by or in the school; otherwise, the educational efforts might be largely wasted.

With the guarantee of an adequate level of physical functioning, the inner-city school is next faced with the fact that more than half of its students suffer from a greatly damaged self-concept, of such magnitude as to interfere or block academic learning. While it is likely that public education in the days ahead will emphasize more and more the acquisition of the tools and processes of learning—learning to learn—it is clear that for inner-city children their predominantly negative self-concepts must be somehow changed into positive ones if they are to find constructive adult roles.

It is also painfully clear that schools generally have failed in this task in the past with this group of children. It is true, as was pointed out earlier, that some of these children do develop success-fully during the school years. Studies of their life histories indicate that there are four rather effective agents in changing their self-concepts. First is the parents who, by their own interests or values or ambitions, can provide the necessary influence. Second is a job; frequently, when a boy gets a job he begins finding self respect and adult identification. Third is marriage; if it is a good one, the sup-port of a spouse and the responsibilities of a home seem to provide a push in the right direction for some. Fourth is the influence of some significant adult outside the family who has established a personal relation to the child. This may be a relative, a neighbor, or sometimes a teacher, in the latter case, one who usually has some contact with a child outside the classroom—frequently through an extracurricular activity.

Middle-class children frequently remember and mention class-room experiences as major impacts on their lives, but the mention of classroom experiences is notably absent in the above list of posi-tive influences for the inner-city child. The development of "the self" must no longer be left to chance or to peripheral activities in the inner-city school; the central activity of the school, namely, the academic program, should be examined for opportunities to im-prove self-concepts of children. The school must change before we can expect the child to change.

The Educational Strategy

The problem can be simply stated: How can a school program be organized for children who may hate school, who have very limited experiences, and who feel like failures, so that they can be helped to discover that they can learn, that learning is fun, that they can see their own successes and develop some feeling of self-worth, that they can respect people and be respected, and that they can see some future for themselves?

These goals are not likely to be achieved by patchwork changes, but rather by imaginative reorganization of school programs. Specific methodologies will best be developed by creative teachers; the discussion below is intended to be suggestive rather than prescriptive, and is mainly concerned with the elementary school.

1. *Pupils must be helped to be active partners in the learning process.*

This is not as innocent a statement as it may sound. In the usual classroom between 70 and 90 per cent of the time will be spent with the teacher talking and pupils listening. This percentage needs to be reversed. The lecture approach, of course, has its time and place, but for these children it is inappropriate. Pupils should participate in the making of every decision possible in their group life. This might include the schedule for the day, the books they are to use, the color of the paint on the wall, the arrangement of the room, or the evaluation of their progress.

Increased pupil participation will undoubtedly mean a major readjustment in the teacher's concept of her own role. A teacher should not be held responsible for having all pupils at any predetermined point of learning on any particular date. Administrators will need to support such a change of expectation, for it is deeply ingrained. Rather, there needs to be a slower and more variable pace, especially with these children.

This does not imply that students run the school or do just what they want to do. It does mean that decision making will be a joint and equal venture between pupils and teacher, one that involves fact gathering, analysis, consideration of alternatives, compromise, and implementation by all parties concerned. Far more time may be spent in making a decision than in the action itself; it may take an entire week to decide about a field trip and only half a day to make it, but the involvement of the pupils in their own future is by far the more important learning experience. This also implies that pupils will be allowed to make poor decisions and live with the results of these decisions; hopefully, learning from mistakes can be channeled into better performance. For instance, in one experimental class of such pupils none had ever participated in any committee work or had ever held a class office. When they decided to have a party, committees were appointed, but they did not do any serious planning of activities for the party or for refreshments. The party was a dud and they all knew it; they were bored and went home early. The planning of a second party was completely different and turned out successfully, with considerable pride felt by all. The usual role of these students in school is passive or resistive; any active involvement is a gain.

2. *Pupils need to learn more from experimentation and from each other than from the teacher directly.*

During most of the school years pupils are more concerned about their relations with their peers than with the teacher or principal. Their worries, hurts, concerns, and satisfactions are centered, to a large extent, in their success or lack of success with the peers that they admire. If this idea is to be pursued seriously, then a restructuring of the classroom program is called for. Classrooms might be organized around small groups of pupils working together, not for just an hour or for a particular project, but as a permanent structure. The work that they do would be more on a problem solving and discovery basis than on teacher-determined assignments. Teachers have worked with small groups over the years, but this implies a different orientation and purpose.

It also implies that school personnel will have adjustments to make. Room furniture will need to be rearranged into small group work centers, and janitors will have to accept the change. Teachers will have to adjust to a higher noise level in the room; they will have to conceive their role more in terms of a consultant working with individuals and small groups rather than controlling classroom processes from the front podium. This means actually shifting at least 50 per cent of the voting stock to the children themselves. Most teachers will feel frightened at this prospect, fearing that discipline will get out of hand and nothing will be accomplished. Needless to say, such changes will have to be made gradually so that the teacher can be assured of pupil progress in assuming responsibility before she grants them more. But, unless this shift of the focus of control actually occurs, there is much less chance for the pupils to participate actively, to learn from their own mistakes, to develop interest in what they are doing—and these are the roads to positive change in the self-concept.

These kinds of procedures are being developed and tested at the present time; more evaluation will be available at a later date (Mental Health Project Grant #535). At this point, however, it is

clear that these classrooms do reach a deeper level of student involvement, that the pupils themselves enjoy school much more, that
they learn more and retain more (as measured by standard achievement tests against a control group), and that they experience more
positive relationships with their peers. Teachers find the first adjustment to this approach difficult, but afterwards they enjoy the new
role to such an extent that they do not care to go back to a former
one. They seem to find a closer relation to students, fewer discipline problems, and more opportunity to relax and move about
the room talking with students. The work referred to has been done
largely at the upper elementary grades, and its applicability to the
early grades is still to be explored.

3. *Curriculum units need to be organized around concrete
experiences, ones in which these pupils can have a high degree of
success.*

The term *cultural deprivation* is based on observations that inner-
city children are deficient in experiences that most children have
in the home during their preschool years. They are deficient in the
ordinary everyday experiences of contact with animal and plant
life, and with neighborhood functions and services out of which
concepts and ideas develop. They are deficient in experiences with
the tools of learning, such as newspapers, conversations with adults,
and books. They are deficient in their human experiences of warmth
and understanding. In the light of such deficiencies, an educational
program will need to provide some of these experiences as a common base for self-expression and intellectual development.

But even more, these experiences will have to be so designed and
timed that they can be mastered by the pupils, who then can experience the pride and satisfaction of success in learning. Such success will depend on the teacher's knowledge of the level of her
pupils, and upon planning the curriculum for where children are
and not for where they should be.

It should be emphasized that here we are talking about curriculum experiences and not extracurricular ones. It is a mistake to
assume that giving Jane errands to run or giving John the responsibility for erasing the board is building a positive self-concept. While
these may be enjoyable to some students, their greatest concerns
are to learn to read and write and figure, and until they feel some
mastery in these areas they are likely to think of themselves as in-

adequate. This is the reason for emphasizing that we need to provide them basic educational experiences in doses that they can assimilate.

4. *Pupils need to be in a classroom atmosphere that is unthreatening, fair, purposeful, and relatively unhurried.*

These seem to be the most important qualities needed within a classroom for maximum personal development and learning. Other qualities could be added to the list, but these seem to be the bare minimum for helping these children attain some of their potential. The teacher aids the development of such an atmosphere by her example in dealing with the children and by her expectation that children will deal with each other in like manner.

5. *Teachers should reduce their evaluative comments in the classroom to a minimum, whether it is expressing praise or criticism.*

Many teachers are prone to use many evaluative comments in the belief that they are quite helpful to children. Some say that children grow as they are given positive criticism and are shown their mistakes. Others believe that praise is the most positive support that they can give children. It is my belief that evaluative comments of any kind inhibit or stop the growth of children. Negative criticism clearly arouses the defenses, and learning is likely to be inhibited for the time being at least. On the other hand, praise may interfere with growth by lulling the individual into self-satisfaction; or if praise is overused, it is ineffective because the child realizes that it means nothing.

These children live in the midst of constant evaluation, most of it negative; they expect evaluation by others, and as long as it is given they will likely continue to accept it. A more adequate self-concept is not only a more positive one, but one that is based on self-evaluation. Teacher comments such as "very good," "no, that's not right," "I like the way you read that," "you can do better than that," all keep the child tied to the teacher's evaluation of him. Praise given to one pupil frequently is interpreted by the other pupils as disapproval of them.

Self-evaluation can be encouraged by questions that invite self criticism by pupils. For example: "Are you sure your problem is right?" "How do you like the picture that you drew?" "What do you like about it?" "Why do you think that?"—these invite self-expression and self-analysis, and growth.

6. *Where possible, teachers should also make their questions to the students requests for their opinion and judgment in preference to requests for the recall of facts.*

The recalling of facts is important, but it does little for developing self-confidence. If the teacher asks for personal opinions and judgments, a student must necessarily put more of himself into the answer, therefore increasing self-development. This is true, however, only if every opinion expressed by every student is given respect and careful analysis, rather than uncritical acceptance or rejection by others.

7. *Teachers must be selected carefully for inner-city schools.*

It is frequently the custom to assign new and inexperienced teachers to inner-city schools because in the school culture these are regarded as the least desirable assignments. This practice is detrimental to both the teachers and the pupils involved. There is some evidence that the most effective teachers in the inner-city are either those who have grown up there and want to return to help children, or teachers who come from the upper-social levels and are less likely to demand that these children behave strictly according to middle-class standards.

One simple way to begin a selection of these teachers would be efforts by the administration to give some status and importance to the job of the inner-city school, and then a request for volunteers to work there. In some way a method must be found for getting teachers who find challenge in this educational problem and who have some of the skills we have referred to.

8. *Some administrative decentralization that would allow the inner-city schools to develop methods, materials, and personnel specifically suited to this child population would seem desirable.*

The differences of this segment of the school population are such that they require different educational programming, and it must be supported by appropriate organization.

9. *To be most effective the school should involve parents in training for helping the children toward more positive self-regard.*

Studies by Brookover and his associates at Michigan State University are indicating, among other things, that when parents are trained in methods of helping their children to improve their self-concepts, greater changes take place than through the use of group counseling or group discussion with the children themselves. Their work was done at the high school level and with other social class levels; however, the implication for the inner-city school seems reasonable. Action programs in New York; Quincy, Illinois; St. Louis; and elsewhere have also found that the involvement of parents is very helpful.

A healthy self-regard and self-confidence is not only a goal of public education, but also a prerequisite to learning. It is as necessary for the middle- and upper-class child as for the slum child, and the discussion in this chapter would apply to all children. However, because of the high incidence of damaged egos in the inner city, improvement of the self-concept becomes a prime target for these educational programs.

At the same time it must be said that the schools can never do the job alone. Unless there are health programs, housing programs, welfare services, and an opportunity for employment as an adult, the chances for progress are slight.

A. Harry Passow

Diminishing Teacher Prejudice

"By all known criteria, the majority of urban and rural slum schools are failures." This judgment by the President's Panel on Educational Research and Development (1964, p. 30) grew out of five indictments of current school practices: the severe scholastic retardation which progressively worsens as children grow older, a dropout rate which exceeds 50 per cent, fewer than five per cent of this group enrolling for some form of higher education, deteriorating IQ scores, and a distressing picture of adolescents leaving schools "ill-prepared to lead a satisfying, useful life or to participate successfully in the community."

The plight of the inner-city school (described in considerable, if depressing, detail elsewhere in this volume) is a pulsing tangle of academic retardation, pupil and staff transiency, racial imbalance, alienation, personnel and staff shortages, and general inadequacy of resources. What still is at issue, however, is the *why* of the inner-city school. The tough question, raised by social psychologists such as Goodwin Watson, is, "To what extent has the school itself cultivated the apathy, lack of self-confidence, absence of persistent effort, the evasions, the suspicions, defensiveness and hostility of slow learners?" (Watson, 1964.) Are the attitudes and biases of professional educators—conscious or not—responsible for the inferior attainments and expression of problems in inner-city schools, or are teachers being made scapegoats for the ills of school and society?

Assessing Cause

The "educational deprivation vs. social deprivation" controversy continues. The former blames the massive academic retardation in depressed areas on the attitudes and behavior of the teachers and administrators; the latter attributes the large-scale underachievement to experiential deficits in early childhood, which fail to equip children to fit into and adapt well to school environments. Difficulties in adjusting to school tasks are predictable but not yet explainable. Both rationales can be supported, and neither alone accounts for the academic malfunctioning in the inner-city school.

Kenneth B. Clark documents the inferior educational attainment of Negro pupils in Harlem's ghetto, but he rejects all explanations under the general heading of "cultural deprivation." Pointing to interview data from HARYOU, he underscores the significance of teacher attitudes in the success or failures of students. Crucial are the problems of white, middle-class teachers in identifying with, accepting, and achieving empathy with children deemed "unappealing or alien." The ghetto school, says Clark, is a scene of educational atrophy and class struggle. Most reprehensible is the practice of placing youngsters in tracks on the basis of invalid judgments of their ability to learn: the consequence is the self-fulfillment of prophecies of uneducability. "They induce and perpetuate the very pathology which they claim to remedy" (Clark, 1965, p. 128).

Even more pointed is Clark's description of the school system wherein power is vested in the hands of white, middle-class professionals:

> The clash of cultures in the classroom is essentially a class war, a socioeconomic and racial warfare being waged on the battleground of our schools, with middle-class and middle-class aspiring teachers provided with a powerful arsenal of half-truths, prejudices, and rationalizations, arrayed against hopelessly outclassed working-class youngsters. This is an uneven balance, particularly since, like most

battles, it comes under the guise of righteousness (Clark, 1965, p. 129).

Martin Deutsch sees minority group and class status as hurting the lower-class child since he "enters the school situation so poorly prepared to produce what the school demands that initial failures are almost inevitable, and the school experience becomes negatively rather than positively reinforced." Deutsch sees experiential differentials as crucial and teachers poorly trained to understand and cope with cultural variations.

> School is an experience which for children in the experimental group (primarily Negro, lower-class children) is discontiguous with the values, preparation, and experience they receive from their homes and particular community; it represents society's demand that they bridge social-class orientations for a few hours a day, five days a week. No catalyst is provided for this transition, and few plans have been made to facilitate the child's daily journey across the chasm (Deutsch, 1960, p. 3).

These formulations by Clark and Deutsch are essentially critical of the predominantly white, middle-class oriented teacher and administrator—of what they do or do not do, of their attitudes and prejudices.

Racial Bias

Philip Freedman asserts that three assumptions can be made about educators, supported by empirical observation, anecdotal data, and common sense—the last two following logically from the first:

> . . . The Caucasian population of the United States harbors a substantial amount of racial prejudice directed against Negroes . . . The teaching staffs of our urban areas, drawn chiefly from the Caucasian, middle-class reservoir, share, in some measure, the negative racial attitudes of the communities from which they spring . . . These negative attitudes impede the participation of the middle-class Caucasian teachers in programs for the deprived child, who is usually either Negro or Puerto Rican.

Freedman maintains that these unhealthy racial attitudes act as a barrier to both the recruitment of teachers for inner-city schools and the effectiveness of teachers assigned to classes consisting of minority group children.

David Gottlieb asserts that, despite considerable attention being given to the problems of racial integration, relatively little data have been gathered about the values, attitudes, and expectations of both Negro students and teachers: "We know even less about the differences and similarities between Negro and white students who find themselves in schools where there are variations in the racial composition of students and teachers" (1963, pp. 2-3).

However, considerable data clarify the consequences of discrimination and segregation on the ego development, motivation, and personality traits of minority group children. David Ausubel, writing particularly about the largest segment of the disadvantaged, the Negro, contends that certain distinctive properties undoubtedly result in significant differences:

> Negro children live in a predominantly lower-class subculture that is further characterized by a unique type of family structure, by specially circumscribed opportunities for acquiring status, by varying degrees of segregation from the dominant white majority, and, above all, by a fixed and apparently immutable denigration of their social value, standing, and dignity as human beings because of their skin color (Ausubel, 1963, p. 109).

Increasingly, educators are beginning to understand the meaning of this background which the Negro child (and his counterpart in every other minority group, with minor or major variations) brings into the classroom from the time he enters. The young Negro is fully aware of racial differences long before he enters school, and much of what goes on in the classroom extends and reinforces his feelings of inferiority. This is so, even when the teacher is basically sympathetic to the problems stemming from discrimination. However, too often teachers and administrators are consciously or unconsciously racially biased, lack understanding and insight into the bases for the child's reactions and behavior, are hostile and frustrated, and think and act in terms of stereotyped images.

On the other hand, Joseph Lohman maintains that most Negroes, as well as whites, think in terms of stereotypes. The Negro child and his parents view the teacher "not as an individual but as a representative of the group which has treated them as inferior and has discriminated against them." While the teacher may in fact be unprejudiced, unless he can accept the pupil's right to these feelings of suspicion and hostility as valid and respond without becoming defensive, he will not be able to serve effectively.

Middle-Class Orientation

Since the studies of the 1930's, the charge has been made that the school is a middle-class institution (Davis, 1948; Hollingshead, 1949; Stendler, 1949; Warner, *et al.*, 1944). From teachers and administrators whose value orientation is middle-class, through a curriculum and teaching materials which reflect the middle-class culture, to modes of discipline and control which are middle-class, the school presents a general climate which rewards and reinforces the behavioral patterns of the middle-class homes. As William Burton (1953) puts it, "The school has generally been geared to the aims, ambitions, moral or ethical standards of the white, prosperous, middle-class, Protestant, Anglo-Saxon population." Further, Burton observes, "Many lower-class children simply do not value the objectives and the processes of the school, hence do not try. The school immediately dubs these children 'unintelligent,' 'uncooperative,' or 'stubborn.'"

Deutsch's study indicated that as much as 80 per cent of the school day in the experimental classes went to disciplining and organizational details (i.e., collecting milk money, cookie funds, reports). In contrast, this figure never exceeded 50 per cent in the control classes. Deutsch suggests that these data imply that the lower-class Negro child is getting one-half to one-third the exposure to learning that children from more favored environments receive and, in all probability, does not get the same help or support at home that is common in the middle-class family. If these findings are consistent, Deutsch speculates, the teacher's role and self-concept are probably transformed from that of an instructor to that of a monitor who is likely to ask for transfer out of the lower-class school as soon as possible (1960, p. 23).

That the social origin of the classroom teacher influences his attitudes toward his pupils, their parents, his colleagues, and the administrators is backed up by several studies. Howard Becker's analysis of social-class variations in teacher-pupil relationships reveals that, by reacting to cultural differences, teachers "perpetuate the discrimination of our educational system against the lower-class child." Becker found that the amount of work and effort the teacher requires varies inversely with the pupil's social class. This aggravates the problem and widens the gap between what the child should know and what he does know in each grade. Children from lower-class families are considered more difficult to control, "being given to unrestrained behavior and physical violence." However, it is in the area that Becker calls "moral acceptability" that the slum child's actions and appearance are most distressing, managing "to give teachers the feelings that they are immoral and not respectable. In terms of physical appearance and condition they disgust and depress the middle-class teacher" (1952a).

Ulibarri's study of teacher awareness of sociocultural differences in New Mexico schools indicates that middle-class oriented teachers:

> Have little awareness of the "life space" of the minority group children in their classrooms. Though these teachers perceived their students' lack of motivation, difficulties with assigned texts, and language deficiences, they did not perceive these problems to be related to differences in cultural backgrounds (Smiley, 1964, pp. 53, 54).

Examining children's perceptions of their teachers' feelings toward them and their self-concepts, scholastic achievement, and behavior, Helen Davidson and Gerhard Lang found a direct relationship between children's social class and teachers' ratings. Also, they found that children clearly sensed their teachers' attitudes toward them; those who felt their teachers ranked them low seemed to have lower self perceptions, achieved less well, and behaved less well in the classroom than did more favored classmates.

By Allison Davis' reckonings, ninety-five of every one hundred teachers are from middle-class origins, a way of life that differs sharply from that of the majority of their pupils. They often undergo an emotional trauma when beginning teaching in situations with lower-class pupils:

> Many new (and old) teachers find it impossible to understand the attitudes and values of these pupils; they are puzzled by the students'

reactions to the material and to the instructor, and by their often sullen, resentful behavior . . . The result in many cases is bewilderment, followed by disillusionment and apathy (Davis, 1964, p. 15).

David Gottlieb reports on the differences and similarities between 36 Negro and 53 white teachers in outlook towards their work and their students (approximately 85 per cent Negro, from low-income families) in six inner-city elementary schools. More than 80 per cent of both groups were female, with the Negro teachers tending to be somewhat younger, more likely to be married, with fewer divorcees or widows. The Negro sample tended to come from larger communities and were twice as likely to have attended public colleges in urban centers. While the white teachers were generally raised in middle-class families, the Negro teachers came from lower-class families, primarily manual occupations. To Gottlieb, the fact that the Negro teachers, more often than the white, came from lower socioeconomic strata, from families headed by a woman, possibly explains the differences in the attitudes and perceptions of the two groups. Gottlieb concluded that white teachers are less-well prepared than their Negro counterparts to work in the inner-city school. With respect to job satisfaction, the Negro teachers seemed less likely to voice their gripes. They tended to mention factors associated with the system (i.e., related to the physical or organizational structure), while the white teachers were more often critical of either students or their parents.

When selecting from a list of thirty-three adjectives those which most accurately described their pupils in the inner-city schools, Negro and white teachers differed in their choices. In order of importance, white teachers most frequently selected talkative, lazy, fun-loving, high strung, and rebellious. Negro teachers selected fun-loving, happy, cooperative, energetic, and ambitious. The white teachers tended to omit adjectives which are universal attributes of children and related to successful learning. Thus, the Negro teacher is less likely to list shortcomings which might be attributed to Negroes generally and point to deficiencies in the system to explain his dissatisfactions. Gottlieb observes:

> The individual whose own educational experience included being part of a middle-class culture where children were "well behaved," fairly sophisticated in the handling of materials and educational

tasks, and socialized by parents who not only played an active role in the school through PTA activities and school-community programs, but saw to it that their children did do their schoolwork, would no doubt experience the greater feeling of "culture shock" when placed in the setting of the inner-city school (1963, p. 9).

Dissonant Standards and Expectations

The effects of social stratification and segregation on the academic attainments of elementary school children have been studied by Alan Wilson, who analyzed achievement records of elementary school pupils in a district characterized by socioeconomic residential segregation. Expecting different achievements among children from varying ethnic and socioeconomic strata, Wilson found also that "the normalization of diverging standards by teachers" crystallized different levels of scholastic attainment. Teachers apparently adapt their norms of success and their concepts of excellence to the composition of their student bodies. They accept much less from the low-income children. The normalization of lower standards of performance in the less-favored socioeconomic group provides the same kind of circular reinforcement for the group that normalization of past performance does for the individual student.

Students who are considered outstanding in less-favored schools do not achieve as high as the average student in the more-favored school, yet receive higher marks. However, as the students progress into secondary schools and junior colleges, uniform achievement criteria are applied to all, and those who have been overevaluated in the past fall behind and often drop out. Wilson observed that students from the "Hills" (more-favored) schools tend to be assigned to the academic streams while those from the "Flats" (least-favored) schools are assigned almost automatically to the general or vocational programs. He also found that although many of the working-class, and especially Negro, students entered the so-called open-door junior colleges, even at this late point they are "counseled or 'cooled out' into terminal vocational training."

Thus, by accepting and expecting lowered standards, teachers must bear some responsibility for the sharp differences between the disadvantaged youth's aspirations and achievements. Wilson comments that whatever educational adaptations need to be made for education of the underprivileged, "misguidance and obscurantism are surely not among them" (1963, p. 234). Arguing that these low expectations and standards on the part of teachers and administrators account for inferior achievement, Kenneth Clark asserts:

> A normal child who is expected to learn, who is taught, and who is required to learn will learn . . . A single standard of academic expectations, a demanding syllabus, and skillful and understanding teaching are essential to the raising of the self-esteem of disadvantaged children, increasing their motivation for academic achievement and providing our society with the benefits of their intellectual potential (1963, p. 157).

But this matter has a second sharp edge. It is easy to see vindictiveness in high standards, as Eleanor and Leo Wolfe caution:

> The dilemma is reflected in the plaint frequently heard from teachers who work in schools in changing neighborhoods. They often report that if they adhere to the same grading standards they used with previous (more privileged) populations they may be accused of prejudice, or at least of harshness, as demonstrated by a larger number of failures and poor grades. But if they alter their grading system, they may be accused of relaxing standards to the detriment of their new pupils (1962).

Perceiving the Job

The unwillingness of new teachers to accept appointments to inner-city schools and the tendency of experienced teachers to seek transfers or to leave teaching have been characterized by Harry Rivlin as a subtle, nationwide teachers' strike which cannot be stopped by a court injunction. The major reason for this condition, Rivlin maintains, is fear:

> They [young teachers] are afraid they will be trapped in a blackboard jungle; they are afraid of possible physical attack; they are afraid that they cannot deal with the situations they will meet in the schools; and they are afraid that they will have to spend their days being policemen rather than teachers (1962).

At Hunter College, Harry Miller found that many education students had a crusading zeal for helping the disadvantaged child, and only a few were hostile. Most were unenthusiastic about the probability that they would be assigned to a difficult school, but accepted it as a fact of life. Whether the student was eager, accepting, or hostile, Miller found that the prospective teacher was unsure and fearful about the forthcoming first assignment: "Newspaper reports, student gossip, their parents' fears, the reports of friends who are already teaching, all have contributed to a body of beliefs about the schools in lower-class areas which build up their general apprehension" (1963, pp. 1, 2).

The high rate of rejection of appointments to depressed area schools by beginning teachers is due, Vernon Haubrich suggests, to the "inability to comprehend, understand, and cope with the multiple problems of language development, varying social norms, habits not accepted by the teacher, behavior which is often not success-oriented, lack of student cooperation, and achievement levels well below expectancies of teachers" (1963, p. 246).

At Queens College, the BRIDGE Project staff found that no matter how much the beginning teacher has read or heard about the low scholastic performance of children in the inner-city school, he apparently has no idea of what this actually means and how it will affect his teaching until he is on the job. The consequence often is a loss of self-confidence on the part of the teacher:

> They are bewildered and desperate, they feel they cannot reach these children, they clutch at the teaching choices mentioned (which their own experience and education contradict), they bitterly submit to a "trainer's" role or misguidedly try a clinician's role, and they no longer have faith that they can be teachers anymore—in these classrooms (Kornberg, 1963, p. 265).

Becker (1952b) found that the typical Chicago teacher's career consisted of shifting from one school to another, seeking a position where basic work problems—stemming from relationships with children, parents, principals and other teachers—were least aggravated and most susceptible of solution. Teachers felt that the nature and intensity of problems vary with the social-class background of the pupils. What comes out by implication is that teachers praise discipline and pliability above their pupils' other traits. The lowest group (slum children) is perceived as "difficult to teach, uncontrollable and violent in the sphere of discipline, and morally unacceptable on all scores, from physical cleanliness to the spheres of sex and 'ambition to get ahead'." Children from the better neighborhoods, on the other hand, are viewed as quick learners, easily taught, but spoiled and lacking such traits as politeness and respect for elders. The middle group (lower-middle and upper-lower class) is perceived as hardworking but slow learning, easy to control, and most acceptable to the teachers on the moral level.

The new teacher in the Chicago system, Becker found, typically begins her career in the least desirable kind of school and then follows one of two paths: she applies for a transfer to a better neighborhood school as soon as possible or she adjusts resignedly over a period of years to the unsatisfactory conditions and work problems of the lower-class school. Adjustment in the second pattern erases the teacher's restlessness and efforts at transfer. A change in the ethnic or racial composition of the neighborhood or in the administrative structure (e.g., arrival of a new principal) may result in the position's becoming unsatisfactory and the teacher's seeking a transfer to a nicer school.

Teaching in the inner-city school is perceived as an undesirable assignment, even as a "type of punishment or an initiation ritual that must be survived if one is to succeed in the city school system." Yet, some teachers do stay and some spend their entire careers there. To find out why, William Wayson studied a sample of forty-two teachers (twenty-seven white and fifteen Negro) who had remained in slum schools and twenty teachers (sixteen white and four Negro) who had transferred from these schools. The most apparent difference between white stayers and leavers was that a greater proportion of the former tended to be inert, rooted in the situation and unwilling to change jobs and face an unknown situation. The second greatest difference was in the liking for the autonomy enjoyed in the slum school—freedom from pressures or interference from outside the classroom, either from parents or administrators. Eighty-nine per cent of the stayers also expressed altruism and loyalty to an accommodating principal who catered to the needs and desires of the staff, while only 19 per cent of the leavers gave responses in one or more of these categories. All Negroes felt constrained by organizational rules and other external pressures, and

their responses tended to agree with those of the white stayers more
than with the white leavers. Wayson also observed:

> Stayers seemingly had internalized the role of teacher (which they
> defined broadly) to a greater degree than leavers (who defined teach-
> ing in terms of academic achievement). Stayers were more personally
> involved in the role and their satisfactions were more ego centered.
> Slightly more of the leavers had experienced shock when they first
> entered the slum school. The greatest shock was caused by the child's
> violation of middle-class standards. The second greatest source of
> shock was the child's inability to perform at the prescribed level of
> achievement.

Simply staying in a slum school cannot be construed as success,
Wayson points out, for other criteria are needed to judge this. Unfortunately, some of the sources of satisfaction for the teacher in the
slum school and some of the reasons for staying seem negative and
unhealthy.

A Better Focus

The foregoing survey of literature gives a bleak montage of teachers and administrators who are blinded by their middle-class orientation; prejudiced toward all pupils from lower-class, racial, and ethnic
minority groups; culturally shocked and either immobilized or punitive in the classroom; and groping constantly for safer berths where
success, in terms of academic achievement, is more likely. Some, not
all, teachers are hostile, vindictive, inept, or even neurotic, but many
more are compassionate and skillful. (Nor are the undesirable teachers found only in inner-city schools.) Even the HARYOU report
(1964, p. 204), which lacerates the schools and their staffs, observes
that "there are brilliant, dedicated, responsible teachers who are
giving children the kind of academic guidelines and exposures which
have made possible a degree of success, in spite of the present structure." Many disadvantaged children *do* achieve; many *do* have
healthy self-images, high aspirations, and positive motivations; for
many, the classroom is the most supportive element in their lives.

The picture of the biased teacher in a school system heavily stacked against the lower-class, minority-group child is both distorted and incomplete. It implies courses of action for the teacher which may be, to some extent, contradictory: to make the classroom a haven from the problems of depressed area living while giving full play to elements of the lower-class culture, to provide many essential social-welfare benefits while still increasing the time devoted to academic instruction. The picture ignores or dismisses as irrelevant the growing body of research which details the impact of poverty and unemployment, of segregation and discrimination, of all other aspects of the inner-city ghetto living on the mental, emotional, and physical development of the disadvantaged child. Having little or nothing to do with policy decisions regarding racial balance and desegregation, for instance, the teacher is called on to implement these policies and to effect integration within the classroom. It is obvious that schools alone cannot deal satisfactorily with all the forces and factors which affect inner-city life—but it is equally clear that the schools (meaning really teachers, administrators, and other personnel) have a central role and a catalytic function to perform.

The classroom teacher creates the curriculm and the climate for learning. The two are, of course, tightly intermeshed. The teacher's attitudes toward and understandings of the inner-city child—a generic term for millions of different personalities—powerfully influence what is learned and the conditions under which it is learned. Concern with educational problems of the disadvantaged has promoted study and modifications of instructional content, teaching methods, resources, school organization, and special services. The elements of *compensatory* and *remedial* programs are being spelled out, although only a beginning has been made. Emerging techniques for diagnosing cognitive and language disabilities of disadvantaged children should help pinpoint curricular adaptations. New publications teach basic skills but they also aim specifically to raise self-confidence among minority groups, enhancing the self-concepts of students and extending understanding and appreciation among diverse cultural groups (Goldberg, 1964a; Passow, 1964). At both the pre-service and in-service levels, teachers need the kinds of experiences which will acquaint them with the potential and applicability of new content, materials, and procedures. But techniques and materials need be accompanied by attitudes composed of such qualities as compassion, respect, reserved judgment, and patience. Writing about the successful teacher of disadvantaged pupils, Miriam Goldberg points out that this teacher:

> does respect his pupils—and not because he sees them through the rose-colored lenses of the romantic—finding "beauty" and "strength" where others see poverty and cultural emptiness. On the contrary, he sees them quite realistically as different from his children and his neighbors' children; yet like all children, coping in their own way with the trials and frustrations of growing up (1964b).

It does little good to belabor the middle-class teacher for having middle-class values; instead, the emphasis must be on knowing about and understanding the lower-class culture, especially when it collides with the culture that permeates our schools. Many of the differences involve relationships, with peers, with adults, with authority figures, with culturally different individuals. The poignancy of Bel Kaufman's heroine in *Up The Down Staircase* (1964) reflects inner conflicts caused by her emotional involvement with her students. Miss Barrett is a teacher who cares deeply about her students, feels and expresses her real warmth toward them, and who is hurt by her inability to reach and be liked by each of her students.

These relationships, involving apathy and withdrawal, aggression and hostility, test the teacher constantly. Joseph Lohman suggests that the teacher must expect and be able to take either rejection or hostility without returning it.

> She is the adult and can expect a little more of herself than of a still maturing student. She must learn to live with frustration and not let it keep her from continued effort. She cannot expect results too soon, either in her own increased awareness of our culturally divergent children or in their reaction to her. She can demand certain standards of behavior; she cannot demand that children trust her or believe in her when they have had too much experience to the contrary (p. 25).

Patricia Sexton argues that middle-class culture, whatever its faults and virtues, differs substantially from lower-class culture. Since the lower-class child has difficulty adjusting to these differences, "we must learn new ways of reaching these groups, and we must provide rules to which they can adjust and rewards which will stimulate their interest in school" (1961, p. 79).

Social and behavioral scientists, together with insightful teachers, have provided analyses of the problems of the inner-city child. But, they have also identified variations from middle-class patterns which can be assets rather than liabilities. Leon Eisenberg advises that "the key issue in looking at the strengths of the inner-city child is the importance of not confusing difference with defect" (1964). Teacher education programs must provide experiences to enable personnel realistically to understand and accept various subcultures, recognizing strengths and positive aspects on which to build. Lohman stresses the need for the teachers

> to understand the cultures from which students come, without viewing the varying cultures as right or wrong, superior or inferior, but simply as different. To the extent that a teacher can really come to understand (not necessarily accept or approve of) the student's subculture, he can come to respect the person from that culture, without necessarily approving of his behavior (pp. 83-84).

The Preparation of Teachers

Clearly, teacher education at both the pre-service and in-service levels needs modification if we are to recruit, train, and keep dedicated teachers who have the know how, insight, and commitment to extend educational opportunities to disadvantaged children. Changes are already being initiated in many teacher preparation programs. One of the more promising is that of Hunter College, whose project prepares teachers in the very school where they will eventually teach. The specific notions being tested by the Hunter program are:

> Student teaching can be both challenging and rewarding in a personal and professional sense; the apprehensions of prospective teachers are best alleviated and their perceptions modified by direct, wide contact with education and community workers and leaders; a team of professionals from the depressed-area school itself—such as subject matter specialists, curriculum experts, and social psychologists

—is required for introducing the student teacher to the particular demands of these schools and for helping orient him to working with children in this special context; participation in a program for teaching in a depressed-area school should be voluntary on the student's part and must begin early in his college career (Passow, 1963, p. 238).

Any teacher program modifications being proposed at this time for inner-city school staffs are concerned with both curriculum and climate—with insights into teaching strategies and content adaptations as well as with understandings of cultural differences. Involvement of subprofessionals, teacher aides, and indigenous persons from the inner city in projects designed to help disadvantaged children has opened up new training programs, some of which have been as helpful for the trainers as for the trainees in altering attitudes toward the culturally different. With support of federal and foundation funds, numerous institutes and workshops have focused on helping staffs plan for integrated education, for preschool programs and for remedial projects of various kinds.

No radical innovations in teacher preparation programs have yet emerged, although some patterns seem to be forming. These include:

(a) Early and continuous contact with children and adults in disadvantaged areas in a variety of school and non-school related activities. These range from one-to-one tutoring of pupils to supervising after-school activities to classroom observations and intensive classroom teaching. These experiences are carefully supervised and often analyzed in seminar or small group sessions afterwards.

(b) Intensive involvement of behavioral and social scientists who apply research and theory from their disciplines to the specific needs and problems of the disadvantaged area. These include cultural anthropologists, social psychologists, architects, city planners, historians and political scientists—many of whom are actively involved in field experiences with students.

(c) Intensive involvement of successful school practitioners—classroom teachers, principals, counselors and others—in working with the teacher education staff in planning, supervising, and evaluating experiences. The two-way flow of college and school staffs has been of considerable benefit to both. Rivlin has urged the use of affiliated schools as laboratories for urban teacher education—drawing the analogy to the teaching hospital attached to the medical school.

(d) Opportunities for pre-service teachers to work with non-school agencies, government and agency-sponsored, and to become actively involved in on-going projects for overcoming poverty, extending civil rights, and generally "reversing the spiral toward futility." Aside from the insights acquired into the life styles of the inner-city families, such experiences are apparently instrumental in more positive attitude formation to the problems faced in such areas.

(e) Modification of college courses to develop those techniques and skills essential to teaching in depressed areas. These include help with diagnostic and remedial procedures, with methods and materials for individualization of instruction, with strategies for classroom control, and with personnel and material resources.

(f) Opportunity to examine, discuss, and plan local program adaptations to known situations, current research, and experimentation being reported by other education centers.

(g) Establishment of internships and other means for continuing relationships between the college and the teacher in-service so that the teacher has continuing supervisory aid as well as support.

Leon Eisenberg maintains that the effective teacher of inner-city children is one whose concern for their welfare goes far beyond the four walls of the classroom: "to citizen participation in efforts to upgrade the neighborhood, to abolish discriminatory practices, to provide more recreational facilities, to support social action for human betterment" (1964). Education in the inner-city school has dimensions which are less crucial in more-favored schools with more advantaged children. Teacher education must offer experiences which will help the teacher, both in preparation and in-service, to modify his behavior and attitudes for the sake of his pupils' healthy and successful learning. In doing so, the teacher will truly teach. Beyond that, as he devotes himself to the many children who are convinced that they have no share in the American Dream, he can help transform the idea of equality of opportunity into reality.

G. Orville Johnson

Motivating the Slow Learner

The term *slow learner,* as generally used, is a misnomer. It implies that the person can learn the same amount and to the same degree as the average individual if he is only given a little more time and a little more repetition. He is slow to learn. In practice this has led to a number of poor and inappropriate educational procedures all designed to bring the slow learner up to grade level. Among the more common methods used are: increasing the length of the school day by keeping him after school; increasing the potential length of school life by retention in grades; and increasing the amount of required practice by assigning additional homework.

Numerous other misconceptions concerning slow learners are also common. They are discipline problems, truants, and delinquents. They are disinterested in learning and in school. They do comparatively better in the special subjects areas than in the academic subjects. They have a short attention span. While all of these characteristics are found more commonly among the school population of slow learners than among the general population of children, they are not innate. The behaviors are, too often, a reflection or result of what teachers and the school have done *to* them rather than *for* them.

The awareness that present-day educators have shown in regard to the slow learners and their desire for help strongly indicates that present procedures have not been satisfactory. Their experience has generally been that the motivation to learn has deteriorated during their years in school rather than increased. Before this trend can be changed, persons responsible for the education of the inner-city slow learners must understand their characteristics and be willing to organize programs and instruction that have meaning and value to them, and also with which they will have success. This may mean abandoning many of the traditional experiences normally provided children as being good and changing basic school administrative structure and organization if this is appropriate.

Slow learners, insofar as the term is used in this section, refers to those individuals who behaviorally appear to be developing intellectually at a somewhat slower rate than is true for average children. Their tested intelligence places them between one and two standard deviations below the mean. Their learning behavior in school is such that even with appropriate instruction and conscientious application their progress in the various areas ranges from three-fourths to nine-tenths of the rate prescribed by standards reflected in the curriculums, courses of study, and textbooks. Present knowledge provides the educator with no known method of increasing this rate of development and thus bringing them up to the norm. Nor will they, in all probability, eventually catch up since their intellectual development appears to cease growing at about the same age that it stops for other persons (Johnson, 1963).

It is essential for educators to operate within the theoretical framework of the previously stated concept since there are no known methods of determining innate or potential intelligence. This concept also provides the teacher with an essential frame of reference to aid him in his development of an understanding of the necessity for slowing down or pacing the instruction.

The individual's rate of intellectual development and unique learning characteristics thus become primary factors influencing both content and methodology. The slow learners are no longer expected to adapt their rate of learning and progress to a predetermined schedule. They are no longer looked upon as having a remedial problem that can be corrected, enabling them to perform according to the dictates of impersonal standards (Johnson, 1962).

The problem of planning programs and instruction for the slow learners that take into account their cultural and experiential backgrounds, their orientation and attitudes toward school-centered learning, their slower rate of intellectual development, and their restricted potential is an interesting, challenging, and important task. It is one that should intrigue and fascinate the teacher of the inner-city classroom. Working on the frontiers of education, he has opportunities for original thinking and planning—opportunities to make his influence felt throughout the community by enabling a population of children to become valuable assets to themselves and to the community rather than liabilities.

Children of the Poor

The educational problem of slow learners is largely centered in schools and classrooms located in low-income neighborhoods. Statistically, one expects that approximately 17 or 18 per cent of the children and youth of the general population will be slow learners. Using this incidence rate, every teacher should expect to average four or five slow learners in every classroom of twenty-five children. Evidence indicates, however, that 80 to 90 per cent of the slow learners reflect a lower social-class background. Economically, the families tend to be either receiving aid from public welfare, or where members of the family are employed, it is at the unskilled, semi-skilled, or service trades level. Educationally (in terms of performance rather than number of grades attended), the parents are often illiterate or, at best, semi-literate. Their living quarters are either an apartment in a community housing project or a flat in a house that is often badly in need of repair and renovation. In many instances the living and sanitary facilities are overcrowded and inadequate, with too many persons residing in too little space. The area of the city is usually considered to be the slums or, in the case of a recent urban renewal program, slated to become the next slums.

These lower social-class persons are often referred to as being culturally deprived or, more recently, socially disadvantaged. Neither of these terms gives an accurate description insofar as providing the essential information necessary to define the educational needs of the children. These needs must be determined before anything approaching an adequate, realistic program that will motivate them to learn can be developed. The basic concepts underlying the terms "deprived" and "disadvantaged" are negative and constricting. These children are disadvantaged only if a qualitative evaluation of "goodness" is placed on any and all activities and experiences considered relatively common to middle-class children. While middle-class values and experiences may be "good" and appropriate for children of middle-class parents, this does not automatically make them the best and most appropriate for children of lower-class parents (Riessman, 1962). Following the concept of deprivation one step further, the experiences these children bring with them to school are inadequate and "bad." Therefore, instruction cannot be built upon these experiences, but rather middle-class ones must be provided so that the children will have a base upon which to build.

The problems of poverty, delinquency, and slow learning are so completely interwoven that it is impossible to deal with only a single facet and solve it without becoming totally involved with the others. Teachers working in the inner city have been frustrated with the lack of results. Too often their efforts appear to have been in vain. This has been primarily due to a basic lack of understanding of what they should and could do with the children. Approximately 40 per cent of the children behave as slow learners (not the expected 17 or 18 per cent) as compared to about 3 per cent in the outlying schools. In terms of relative numbers of children alone, these teachers must be much more aware of the problems posed by the slow learner, much more knowledgeable in reference to the educational implications, and much more willing and able to make curriculum changes and instructional adjustments than is necessary for teachers in general.

Many modern teacher preparation programs, particularly those concerned with training primary and elementary school teachers, devote a great deal of time discussing ways and means of motivating children to learn. It almost appears as if learning were an activity foreign or alien to human nature and some artificial means must be used to encourage children to participate. This being assumed for children in general, it must be true to even a greater degree for children who are having difficulty learning the material presented—children such as these slow learners.

Children generally, including the slow learners, are curious and anxious to learn. They want to know about things; how to do things, to do the same things other children are doing, to grow up. Since most persons in the broad American society can read, write, compute, and have certain knowledges concerning their physical and social environment, in order to belong and to be similar to other persons, one must have somewhat similar abilities and values to get along in the general community with a minimum of friction.

The slow learner entering the inner-city classroom also wants to "know how to read" initially, and later how to do these other things. He defines his educational goals in much more specific terms than does the educator who mouths the objectives stated by the Educational Policies Commission of the National Education Association. But, he comes to learn. It is only after he has been subjected to numerous failures and becomes frustrated over his inability to learn from the instruction he has been receiving that he finally adopts the façade of "Who cares?" Then, instead of his having an internal motivation to spur him on to new learnings, the teacher finds it necessary to resort to artificial means of regaining his flagging attention and interest.

A number of factors are commonly present within the inner-city schools that reflect the apparent lack of general community awareness or desire to support quality education for the slow learners. While many of the buildings that house the classes these children attend are old, since they are often the ones built when the community was much younger, if they are still structurally sound there is no excuse for lack of modernization, renovation, redecoration, and adequate lighting, supplies, and equipment. Too often these schools and classes are apparently used as proving grounds for new teachers and administrators. Successful ones (those who can survive and keep the "roof nailed down") are promoted to "better" schools. The less adequate tend to remain. The resulting mediocre instruction, the general lack of attention to and study of these children's educational problems, and second-class equipment and facilities have generally mitigated against the development of meaningful programs for the slow learners.

Directions for Action

Three fundamental things (other than the mechanical improvement of physical plants and provision of essential equipment and supplies) must be done to correct the present situation: (1) quality educational personnel must be selected to teach the classes and supervise and administer the programs; (2) curriculums and courses of study must be planned that take into account the child's environmental background, learning abilities and characteristics, and academic, social, and occupational potential; and (3) methods and techniques must be adopted that will ensure continuous success in their learning the skills and content included within the curriculum.

The only way in which the motivational problem can be solved is through the provision of an appropriate program and adequate instruction. If the problem is corrected early in the child's school life, motivation will never be absent. If the correction is made during the upper elementary years, extraneous motivating devices will probably be required. If uncorrected or not corrected until the secondary school level, it is probably too late to salvage them. The slow learners, the truants, the discipline problems, the early dropouts, the poorly trained adults inadequately prepared to cope with the demands made by the community are too often the result.

Quality Educational Personnel

The single most important factor in determining the quality of a program is the competence of the personnel responsible for it. Teachers and administrators and supervisors should be carefully selected upon the basis of their competence and a healthy interest in the educational problems of slow learners. Often teachers are assigned a group of slow learners upon a rotating basis. Since their primary interest and orientation is in reference to more traditional kinds of programs and instruction ordinarily provided children, they have little or no desire to put forth the necessary effort to learn about and do something constructive in program development for the slow learners. These teachers will not be responsible for educating the same group next year, and their primary objective seems to be to get through the present year. This kind of assignment may also generate a great deal of hostility in the teacher toward the slow learners. He resents having to be subjected to them even for a year.

The assignment of less adequate teachers to the program is also self-defeating. The attitude that "using teachers who cannot teach for children who cannot learn" as an ideal solution for problems posed by tenure laws is completely untenable. Something more than partially warm bodies is required for these classes.

Teachers of the slow learners must be emotionally stable, healthy persons who see working with slow learners as an interesting and challenging activity. They must derive their satisfactions from gradual changes in behavior and attitudes and slower growths in knowledge and skills rather than from the academic honors normally obtained by brighter students. They must have an empathy with the slow learners and be able to recognize and understand their problems. There is no place for emotional sympathy or a desire to be a parent substitute. They must be willing to accept the children while still not necessarily accepting or approving their behavior. They must be willing to become personally acquainted with them, their parents, and their environment, and then translate this information into a meaningful program that will enable the children to cope with their problems more effectively than if the program had not been provided. They must be willing to make an effort to extinguish much of their previous learnings and attitudes developed as a result of their own home and neighborhood environments, their own schooling, and the instruction they received in their teacher preparation programs. They must be willing and capable of applying basic principles to the development of sound programs specifically designed for the slow learners.

Similar requirements and demands are both appropriate and essential for the supervisors and administrators responsible for these programs. Teachers must be organized and helped to work together so that continuity and progression is provided in the program. In order to accomplish its purpose, the program must be a total one with the teachers at each level aware of the experiences that have been provided the children at an earlier date and also the experiences that will be following. Any gaps will destroy much of the potential value of previous learnings and may prohibit the reestablishment of the necessary motivation essential to encouraging the child to complete the training of which he is capable.

Where necessary, the structure of the educational program should be redesigned. The program should not be expected to fit into or adapt to traditional, preconceived structure or organization. Rather, structure should be designed to facilitate and encourage efficient instruction and an effective program.

When the selection and training of teachers, the development of program, and the total school structure is organized around the slow learner, for the slower learner, the instruction becomes appropriate and meaningful. No unique problems of motivation can arise. The entire question regarding the encouragement of motivation in the slow learner becomes important only when this is not done.

Curriculums and Courses of Study

Numerous gimcracks and fancy materials have been introduced into education during the past two or three decades. These have, hopefully, been designed to attract and maintain the interests and to motivate the reluctant learners. No automatic indictment of all methods, materials, and equipment that has been introduced into education within the last generation is intended. On the other hand, educators should be somewhat wary of manufacturers' claims and the blind acceptance of anything and everything new as being good merely because it is new. This includes the "modern math" programs for which great claims have and are being made. Mathematicians are not in universal agreement concerning the values generally, to say nothing about appropriateness for slow learners, and some findings indicate certain shortcomings and limitations are present.

Many of the more recently introduced materials, curriculum changes, and methods, however, are excellent—far superior to those they have replaced. For example, books are made much more attractive through better illustrations, and have more controlled content with systematic introduction of new materials. The educational toys and materials used at the preschool and primary grade levels display improved design and are "dressed up" to be more attractive than those previously used; such as the relatively drab and unexciting form boards. Numbers of excellent visual aids have added a potentially valuable new dimension to education for the encouragement of motivation and consequent learning. These may prove to be potent instructional tools for use with the slow learners. Modern laboratories for experimentation and science displays and demonstrations have tended to take instruction into visual learning and learning through active participation in the activities, replacing the verbal type heretofore used almost universally.

These and the myriad of other new things that have been added to modern classroom instruction have proved to be excellent for initial motivation and instruction for the average and the college-bound student. The continuing high dropout rate among the slow learners is ample evidence, however, that they have not provided the essential ingredient for the maintenance of continued interest and motivation for them. The reasons are relatively simple, and upon examining them the educator should obtain some clues concerning the appropriate course of action that must be followed.

First, some of the materials, such as many of the primary grade readers, reflect a middle-class orientation that is completely foreign to the slow learners residing in the inner city. The suburban residence, the children's activities, the family relationships, and the entire value structure forming the story background have little or no meaning to them. This does not mean that new materials must be written that reflect a lower social class background and bias, but "classless" materials concerned with animals, fables, and so forth would undoubtedly be more appropriate.

Second, the curriculum is, in general, identical for all students regardless of background or ability. (The exceptions are the programs organized for the educable mentally retarded.) The curriculums were originally designed for the potential college student. Modern curriculums are largely adaptations of these earlier programs based upon the concept that a broad liberal arts experience is good and therefore appropriate for all children. No concerted effort has been made to conscientiously reject or repress traditional thinking in the area of curriculum development and plan for the educational needs of specific, unique groups of children.

Third, the public school has been primarily thought of as being preparatory for more specific training at a later date—college, business school, or vocational training. Yet, for the slow learners the public school must be thought of as being terminal for the majority of them. Programs for them must be planned accordingly.

The curriculum of the public school in general can be divided into two basic groups or areas—the skills and the content subjects. The special subjects (art, music, physical education, and so forth) provide instruction in both areas to a greater or lesser degree. The fundamental skills commonly included, and equally necessary for the slow learners, are communication (listening, speaking, reading, language, spelling, and writing) and the understanding and ability to use quantities and quantitative relationships. This part of the curriculum for the slow learners deviates relatively little from that provided all children, except in extent and depth.

Skills. Modern society requires that each person have a basic minimum of academic skills. This is essential if he is to become a contributing citizen and function effectively within society. The higher the level to which these skills are developed, the easier it is for the individual to adjust to the demands of the physical and social environments and the greater the number of choices available to him in regard to the selection of the role he will be able to assume. The illiterate is far more limited in his selection of jobs and social experiences than the high school or college graduate.

Slow learners, because of their slower rate of intellectual development and limited final level of ability, will never be able to achieve in academic skill areas to the degree expected of average children. They will be ready for formal instruction approximately one year later and their final achievement level can realistically be expected to be that normally assigned to the junior high school age child. This does not, however, provide a legitimate excuse for failure to include instruction in these skills. A person functioning effectively at this level has command of the essential tools required to perform in semi-skilled and skilled job areas with the benefit of some additional vocational training.

Since the slow learners are faced with the problem of having somewhat limited intelligence and potential achievement, it is essential that the schools ensure that they learn as near to their ability levels as possible. Persons with average or superior intellectual ability may be able to get by not performing at or near their ability levels. If this occurs with the slow learners with their relatively meager abilities, they may become social misfits and economic dependents.

The basic skills essential to effective communication and the ability to use quantitative concepts are the fundamental tools required for the adequate performance of normal daily living activities: obtaining information, expressing needs, continuing to learn, and dealing with the innumerable quantitative relationships demanding a minimum ability level in the skills and a knowledge of

basic concepts plus the ability to use them. These needs are as prevalent in the common everyday life of the slow learners of the inner
city as they are among persons performing at a higher level who
reside in the suburbs. The only differences may lie, and then only to
a limited degree, in the kind and extent of the problems facing these
respective groups.

The slow learners, like other children, understand these are considered important, that adults generally make continuous use of
them, and that other children are taught them and that they learn
them. As a result, they enter school with a desire to learn—not how
to get along with Johnny, nor to be civic-minded citizens, but to
learn to read, write, and do arithmetic. The motivation to learn is
present; if they are taught these skills and how to use them as tools,
there will never be any motivational problems. What they are being
taught is valuable, it has meaning and purpose, and they are having
success in their attempts to learn it. The school itself must accept the
primary responsibility, in most instances, when interests lag and
motivation to learn is no longer present.

A common complaint of teachers is that they have no educational
materials designed for these slow learners. Some educators who
agree with them have suggested as a result that each teacher prepare his own. No teacher has the time, and few, if any, have the
necessary training to prepare developmental instructional materials
that will ever equal, to say nothing of surpass, the quality of com-
mercially-prepared texts, workbooks, and so forth. In actuality, no
commercial materials are designed to provide for the instructional
needs of all children, or even of one child. They are designed for
the statistically average child who does not exist. The content is inappropriate for one, the pace is too slow for another, and the material is presented too rapidly for a third. The materials, however, are
usually well organized and presented in relatively appropriate
sequence. As a result the good teacher makes the necessary adaptations by skipping material, going over other material rapidly, and
preparing or finding supplementary materials, depending upon the
intellectual and academic development of the child, and also taking
into account his experiential background as it is related to the topic
at hand. The same approach is essential if the slow learners are to
obtain adequate instruction and thus derive any benefit from their
education. But the necessity for new or unique materials insofar as

learning in the skill areas is concerned is not indicated. Select the best ones that are available and use them intelligently.

Content. The primary content areas, specifically the sciences and social studies, present problems that are quite different from those posed by the skill areas. Here the sequence of difficulty of understanding and learning has not been as well established. Much of the material taught has little or no meaning or value to the slow learners of the inner city (at least at the time it is presented). The content is often based upon a background of experiences they have not had either directly or vicariously. Again, teachers complain that little or nothing is available for these children. This time the complaint is a more valid one than was true for skill instruction. The identical problem, however, is true for the vast majority of the children of the inner city and is not confined to the slow learners. The question is, then, "What does one do about it?"

On far too many occasions the textbook controls the curriculum rather than being selected as the result of providing the materials appropriate for the defined program. In the present case the process must be reversed. Committees of teachers, working with similar kinds of children who reflect similar kinds of backgrounds and environments, must be organized to study their curriculum needs in sciences and social studies. From this investigation a course of study should develop that will guarantee the children will have the essential information, knowledge, and understanding that will ensure that they will be able and willing to cope with their physical and social environment effectively—now as children and later as adults.

The formal science program of biology, chemistry, and physics of the classical senior high school has little or no value for these slow learners. Many of the concepts included in these courses as well as the ones contained in the general science course and the elementary science program, however, do have value and should be taught. As a result, a different science curriculum incorporating all of the things of value and excluding those things of little or no value must be developed.

The identical basic deficiencies and strengths briefly pointed out in regard to science programs for slow learners also obtain in the case of social studies. An emphasis upon the immediate is most appropriate because they tend to be less mobile than the rest of the population and also tend to be less active citizens of the community.

They vote less often, are less aware of their civil rights as well as their civic responsibilities, and tend to carry less than their share of the load in contributing to the solution of community problems. Intensive study of the nature of the community, social and civic agencies, government, laws, and so forth, and their relationship to them is essential. Far less emphasis need be placed upon national and international places and problems than is true for normal children.

The area of the social sciences probably illustrates more clearly than any other area the necessity for individual community planning of programs. When general or even state curriculums are recommended, they can reflect no specific community characteristics, problems, and situations. For example, the various problems facing a person living and growing up in New York City are unique and distinct from those faced by a similar person residing in Los Angeles, Houston, or Minneapolis. Even the problems within a large city, such as New York, may vary greatly from one area to another—the Bronx to Brooklyn to Staten Island. Programs, to be most meaningful and to have the maximum value, must be concerned with the problems of the children enrolled in them. In addition, these programs must be alive and subject to change as the society and general environment change. Thus, a curriculum is never finished. It is serving its purpose best only when it is under continuous study and being changed as the nature of the community changes.

Special Subjects. The special subjects areas are fully as important for the slow learners as they are for normal children. They provide added experiences in a number of valuable ways, enabling the individual to communicate using a wider variety of methods, developing a more efficient and usable body, and learning about numerous media, techniques, and tools that will increase personal effectiveness and understanding of his environment. No one of these subjects is either appropriate or essential to every slow learner. Each child must have his individual program planned specifically based upon his characteristics and his educational needs.

Art, music, and work with various construction media are examples of potential activities in the non-verbal expression areas. Physical education is important in the development of a more efficient physical machine and for vocational or recreational purposes. Industrial arts and home economics have daily practical application as well as being potentially valuable as an introduction into the vocational areas. In the development of an effective human being, all these experiences can and should be used.

Methodology. Teachers often request that they be given some unique method or technique to use with their slow learners, expecting that somehow this will miraculously solve all the educational problems posed by this group. If this does not make them learn like normal children, at least it will change their interests and general behavior in a positive manner and at the same time provide a solution to the problems posed by their apparent lack of motivation. Unfortunately, the answer is not that simple and the panacea not that easy to obtain. A better understanding of the psychology of behavior, including learning, on the part of the teachers, and a better application of the principles that are known is required (Ingram, 1960).

The following are a number of important principles that are often violated. These violations, along with the use of inappropriate content, have, to a large degree, been responsible for the present dilemma. The ultimate result has been the large number of behavior problem, truant, uneducated, relatively illiterate, and early school dropout slow-learning youth of the inner city.

Readiness. The principle that is probably violated most commonly in teachers' attempts to instruct these slow learners is that of readiness (Kirk, 1940). Too often there appears to be a complete lack of awareness that there is a readiness for all learning whether it be skills, content, attitudes, or social behavior. The readiness that is familiar to most educators (at least as a term) is that of reading readiness. Yet, as these words are used and the concept singly applied, one wonders whether or not the teachers are aware that these are two words—reading readiness.

Primary teachers and reading specialists have long recognized that certain skills must be developed, certain experiences experienced, and a certain level of intellectual maturity achieved before a child will probably have success with learning to read. Even here, with standardized tests available designed to measure a child's level of readiness, too often it is ignored.

A commonly accepted statement, one that has almost become a truism, is that these slow learners have little or no interest in learning. Their primary objective in life, dating from the day they were enrolled in school, is to get out as soon as possible and to do so by exerting as little effort as possible. Initially, the slow learners enter kindergarten or first grade, like all children, desiring to learn. Their primary objective is to learn to read. When teachers are unaware of the slow learners' somewhat retarded intellectual development (they look normal) and they have no background that enables them to make an identification, they provide these children with the same instruction as the other children in the class. But, the slow learners are not ready.

Far too often it is assumed that all children who have lived a specified number of years are equally prepared to benefit from identical instruction and, therefore, appropriately belong in the same class or grade. Nothing could be farther from being true. The slow learners from the inner city have at least two strikes against them. One, they have not had many of the extra-school experiences upon which much of the middle-class oriented instruction (including the textbooks and materials used) is based. Seldom has the instruction been changed to take advantage of or to build upon the experiences they bring with them to the classroom. Too, their retarded rate of intellectual development places them at a lower level of intelligence than that for which the graded instruction was designed as long as "social promotion" policies are in effect.

After a child has been initially motivated to learn, that is, the child understands the value and purpose of the learning activity, it is essential that he have success. As a result, his initial desire for and interest in learning will continue. This success can be achieved only if he has the required background information and skills as well as a sufficient level of intelligence to learn it. When instructing the slow learning children of the inner city, teachers must be aware of the experiences the children bring to the learning situation, their somewhat retarded intellectual level, and their slower rate of intellectual development. The consideration of these factors will ensure their readiness for the learning tasks being presented today and will also provide that the pace of the instruction is such that the children will continue to be ready for each successive learning—tomorrow, next month, and next year.

Teach Directly. Much of the instruction that is provided children today, particularly at the elementary level, is of an integrative nature. The experience unit is a commonly used method for accomplishing this. The purpose of this kind of instruction is to help children understand the interrelationships of the skills and the content areas. Unfortunately, it is easily used in such a manner that the slow learners have little or no understanding of what they are supposed to be learning. By having the reading, arithmetic, writing, and spelling activities all centered around a central topic or theme, the child may be devoting all of his energies to learning about the topic and derive little or no benefit from the incidental skill instruction he is receiving. In other words, he does not realize that he is receiving instruction in reading or arithmetic and as a result does not learn the subject matter.

Another limitation of this method of instruction, seldom if ever mentioned by its proponents, is the general lack of developmental materials available relating to the content of the selected topics. As a result, skill instruction tends not to be systematic. Yet, this is essential in the teaching of new skills, the introduction to successive steps of a skill, and the provision of regular reinforcement of the skill to reduce forgetting.

There is some evidence to indicate that a direct instructional approach has the greatest value for these slow learners. That is, when reading is being taught it should be taught as reading, using the best developmental reading materials available. The children should be fully aware that this is a reading lesson and then taught to read. This would also be true of the other skills included in the program.

The experience unit should not be rejected as an instructional device, however. It has real value if used correctly. A unit is usually related to some problem in the social studies area. It thus provides instruction related to this important topic. But, to be most effective it should be selected from an experience common to all of the children. In many instances, pre-experiences fulfill this requirement. Though common, appropriate experiences are not universally present in the children's living; a class experience with necessary preparation or an excursion is easily provided. The purpose of the unit, insofar as the skill areas are concerned, is to initially demonstrate the need for and develop the basic concepts related to the use of the skill. Here the unit is a tremendous aid because it places the learning in a concrete, socially meaningful context. By having the instruction of the basic concepts placed in relation to a previously meaningful situation, the student is able to learn the principle involved more easily.

The final value of the unit is to provide the student with numerous near-life situations in which he can use the skills and apply the principles learned. In this way the probability that the children will become more and more able to correctly apply and use the skills as the occasion demands is significantly increased. The skills have little or no value in and of themselves. Their value lies in their efficient and effective application.

Use Developmental, Systematic Instruction. This principle of instruction might well be considered a corollary to the principle of readiness. All instruction should be provided at the developmental level of each child or when he is developmentally ready. When material (skill or content) is taught developmentally, it is also taught systematically. But, systematic instruction is not necessarily developmental—the readiness of the individual must determine the level and rate.

It is essential that each step of instruction be carefully planned and presented to the slow learners. This will ensure that there are no gaps necessary for him to fill independently. In this way he will be kept at or near his maximum ability level at all times. Where gaps are left, a future level of intelligence may be required on the slow learners' part that they will never attain. The educator cannot afford to take this chance. The slow learners must be performing as efficiently and at as high a level as possible when they leave school. There is not a sufficient amount of intelligence available for them to be performing at anything less and still have the effectiveness to be of value to themselves and to society.

Teach for Transfer. An old saying that has been too often accepted is that the slow learners and the mentally retarded are particularly deficient in their ability to generalize and to learn and apply a principle. Entire programs have been developed based upon this hypothesis. Realistically, it is impossible to even list, to say nothing about teaching every child, all the social, vocational, and other things they are going to need throughout their entire lives. Not only is the list too long, but the society and the economy are changing so rapidly that it is impossible to predict the kind of world in which one will be living one, five, or ten years from now.

The latest information concerning the intellectual characteristics of the slow learners seems to indicate that their deviation from the normal is primarily in terms of amount rather than kind (Johnson,

1963). Thus, they can generalize and apply principles toward the solution of problems, at least to the level of their measured intelligence. Therefore, it behooves the educator to provide them with sufficient basic skills that they will continue to learn following the termination of their formal schooling and sufficient information upon which to build. In this way they will be able to change and adjust to a changing world. They will become adjustable rather than adjusted individuals.

Education is for the present and based upon present characteristics, present abilities, and present needs. It is impossible to predict the future specific needs of even one individual, to say nothing about the needs of a group. Even if this were possible, instruction of a skill or of information important at some vague future date would have been largely forgotten and consequently useless when the time eventually came for its application. Furthermore, the instruction would have little or no value to the individuals because adulthood is a long time off for children. With no purpose there is little or no incentive or motivation to learn.

While the educator does not teach for the future directly, he has a great deal of influence upon how the individual will behave in the future. He provides the slow learners with experiences that help them become more effective ten-year-olds when they are ten years of age and more effective fifteen-year-olds when they are fifteen years of age. He realizes that the quality of citizenship shown by today's sixteen-year-old largely determines what he will be at seventeen. But, in addition, the educator must also provide his students with the basic tools and knowledge to continue to learn and continue to grow in a desirable direction.

One word of caution. While the vast majority of the inner-city slow learners drop out of school at as early an age as possible under present conditions, this should have no effect upon the program they take up to that time. The educational experiences they will miss cannot be filled in at an earlier date. This is a very tempting thing to try but should be resisted. They must be given the foundation for these later experiences so that if they have the ambition and ability to acquire them by themselves they may do so, or if they should return to school they will be ready to continue with the terminal part of the program. The ultimate solution, of course, is the provision of programs that will hold more and more of these slow learners until they are ready to leave.

Special Methods. Investigations, primarily with educable mentally retarded children but reflecting the same experiential backgrounds as the inner-city slow learners, have indicated no unique learning characteristics. Thus, there are no special techniques that will magically solve their educational problems. No unique methodologies are generally recommended. Some studies, however, seem to imply that children who are raised in a somewhat meager verbal environment may derive greater benefit from visual instruction than from the more commonly used oral instruction. Since these slow learners may tend to be somewhat deficient in the verbal areas, it might prove worthwhile to introduce more visual materials and demonstrations into their instruction and reduce their dependence upon understanding orally presented materials.

Another area worthy of trial and experimentation is the use of well organized, programmed instruction materials. This systematic, step-by-step presentation of instruction is highly recommended for these children. This systematic approach is a primary characteristic of programmed materials and may provide at least a partial answer to some problems involved in the instruction of slow learners.

Summary

The problem of motivating the slow learners has become one of particular importance in recent years (Featherstone, 1951). As the society and economy have become more complex, it has become increasingly apparent that the citizens must perform at higher levels in order to cope with the every-day problems of living. That substantial numbers of the slow learners have not been motivated to learn to perform adequately and acquire sufficient skills and knowledge to deal appropriately with problems arising from their environment has become apparent to both laymen and educators. This lack has been forcefully demonstrated in a number of ways—the high incidence of school dropouts, the relatively large number of marginal and total illiterates among native adults, the increase of "hard core" families continuously receiving public assistance, and the high incidence of crime and delinquency among certain teenage groups and young adults.

Although the problems posed by the slow learners have faced educators since the turn of the present century, it is only since World

War II that anything approaching a concerted effort has been directed toward the discovery of a solution. The majority of the earlier efforts were largely mechanistic in nature. Attempts were made to discover whether or not there was a better means of grouping the children for instruction, or special techniques or methods of instruction were sought. Neither of these approaches proved to be very effective.

In order to motivate the slow learners so that they will desire to obtain the education of which they are capable and to remain in school until they have obtained it, one must become concerned with the very foundations of education. First, a program must be planned and articulated that will provide these children with meaningful experiences that have real value to them.

Second, basic psychological principles of learning must be practiced when providing the instruction to ensure they will have success in learning the skills and content taught. The most important of these principles is that of readiness. The process is essentially circular in nature. The material is of value to the learner. He has success in learning it. His initial interest not only continues but increases. He then applies himself more diligently and learns even more. Motivation is present and intrinsic.

Finally, the administrative structure of the school must be so organized as to promote learning and enable essential instruction to take place as efficiently as possible.

Paul R. Hunt and Elvin I. Rasof

Discipline: Function or Task?

Traditionally, and by design, the school with its mission to mold, strengthen, and perfect operates within a syndrome of discipline. Discipline has been and continues to be both a function and a task of the school. To the extent it becomes more or less of either is determined, by and large, through what is described to be the mission of the school and, moreover, through the style with which teachers and administrators interpret their roles in relation to the school's mission.

Although not enough may be known about discipline in public schools serving medium-income families and above, those reading this chapter will, for the most part, be products of such schools. Therefore, the reader will have some appreciation for the system of penalties and rewards as they relate to middle-class respect for discipline. Moreover, if those reading this chapter are to become teachers, they will carry with them into the classroom a whole system of expectancies that hinge almost completely on their concept of discipline as it operates through middle-class functions and tasks.

The newly assigned teacher, if reporting to a school much like the one he or she attended during both elementary and secondary years, will, to a great extent, be in tune with the school environment. Given a set of circumstances and clues, the teacher can establish expectancy levels and anticipate the behavior of his charges; thus, teacher and student can *read* each other.

This, however, may not be the case for the middle-class teacher who accepts an assignment in a school serving very low-income areas. It is, then, to the teacher and administrator who may be working with children in such circumstances the following remarks are addressed.

Before introducing observations as to how children from very low-income areas behave and how this behavior may give rise to both the function and task of discipline, the reader should be asked to examine his concept of discipline. More than likely, the term conjures up a punitive connotation and fails to give rise to other appropriate meanings. Through examination of the term, however, one is soon reminded that discipline often carries less threatening meanings. For example, much of the middle-class reward system, through which many pleasures are derived, comes from self-imposed discipline. This example, like others familiar to the reader, should be kept in mind as tasks and functions of discipline are considered (Reissman, 1953).

The Inner-City Child

Because the school is usually an embodiment of the supporting society, the inner-city child, by comparison, is different. In addition, he is poor by definition (either the family income is below a specified norm, or the family income falls within an arbitrarily determined percentage of the population), a misplaced minority of his social stratum (60 per cent of the American poor *do not* live in the inner city or the suburbs), and a cause for concern to educators everywhere (Morgan, 1962). Being *different* has many implications, not the least of which is belonging to a class that is different from his teachers'. As in the usual case, the inner-city child is taught by a teacher from the middle class, and conversely, the teacher comes in contact with the inner city through its children. In a fashion analogous to Mr. Gagus, who lived in Brooklyn but spent his working hours as doorman of the "Greatest Picture Palace in the World . . . dressed as a Captain of the Grenadier Guards of the First Empire," the inner-city teacher lives in one world that is real, and visits one world which can be almost make-believe. On the other hand, as in the Oriental fable of the man who upon waking did not know whether he had dreamed he was a butterfly, or whether he was a butterfly dreaming he was a man, the inner-city teacher is bound to reach a point where he is not sure which of his two worlds is real.

More likely than not, this teacher has not volunteered to enter the inner-city school—although the trend is changing—and when confronted with the business of teaching finds that many of the textbook techniques ("look at, or stand near, the offender," "request a parent-teacher interview," "appeal to fair play and good manners," "corporal punishment," etc.) are not always applicable. Further, to a person raised in a different cultural element, low-income problem students seem to handle life in a way that does not usually make sense. For example, making a promise of a reward for being good is much less appealing to children living in the slums—not that such children do not like rewards and that their teachers do not like to extend such favors. Mr. A., wanting to do something extra, promised a Christmas party to his class if they would behave in the lunchroom for the month of December. After two days of angelic comportment, the class reverted to its ebullient normalcy. Thwarted by his students' reluctance to "merely" behave in return for such an "exorbitant" reward, Mr. A. was appalled to find the class expecting "at least" cookies in return for the two days. Herein lies an example of how each may differ in what they consider to be good behavior. To the teacher, the class had reneged by not fulfilling its contract; to the students, the good behavior was elicited by the promise of a bribe and a portion of one deserved a portion of the other. Often the child is not called upon in his environment to differentiate between those things which, in the eyes of his middle-class teacher, are distinctly good and bad. Mr. A., refusing to accept the class's seemingly minuscule effort, was rewarded for his good intent with daily resistance. How easy it is for the child to appear as resentful and undisciplined when any breakdown in communication occurs (Estvan, 1959; Educational Policies Commission, 1962).

Two Axioms

Two axioms are then present: (1) The classroom teacher, by virtue of his environmental field, differs from his students in perceptions, feelings, and actions, and (2) The classroom teacher is not fully prepared to deal with many of the unexpected actions commonly found in inner-city schools.

One theorem which may well be deduced is that most teachers new to inner-city schools experience great difficulties in fulfilling what they perceive to be their professional responsibilities. When faced by the twin horns ("function" and "task") of the dilemma of discipline, they tend to recreate the environment from which they come and consequently inculcate upon the child's already "distorted perception of life" the schism between life in the street and life in the school. As an illustration, consider the teacher's major function in the classroom. If it is not to teach, then why the title "teacher"? And yet many teachers expect the discipline of a monk (observe your own fellow classmates the next time a test is returned to them —it is only natural to want to talk and compare papers, and who can be absolutely quiet while passing out textbooks?), the respect due an Olympian god (do you respect all of your instructors?), the obedience of a trained artist (remember that many slum children have no one to obey and consequently have not learned this "skill"), and the tolerance of a saint (live and let live) (Conant, 1961).

A corollary to this theorem is that the teacher will eventually reach a level of competency and comprehension of the function and task of discipline, within the philosophy of his school and school system, that is acceptable to himself, the students, and the school. And yet, the fact remains the majority of teachers who are new to inner-city schools are unhappy with their disciplinary prowess and/or request transfer to another school or system. But what about the many teachers who do succeed in the inner city and would never think of leaving? What are their secrets and how can the inexperienced teacher effectively adopt and utilize them? For example, is discipline always a task to perform or is it merely a function of good teaching? What are the means of preventing trouble before it happens, and how does one correct trouble after it happens?

Attitudes of the Inner-City Child

Many inner-city children appear resistant, hostile, and suspicious. They have gross distortions with regard to their concept of independence, problems with authority figures, and have a superficial relationship with their peers. Outside of the classroom, many children have little or no contact with adults who have the interest or the time for them. Often adults living in very low-income areas are found to be gloomy, silent, mechanical, and lacking in spontaneity. They are not equipped to respond to the curiosity of the child. Rather than tolerate the child's natural curiosity, it becomes a threat, and they will often resort to punitive methods. Sometimes, when the classroom becomes a symbol of failure and frustration, children, having been groomed to conform and respond to irrational methods, unconsciously tease their teachers into using similar methods in managing the discipline problems in the classrooms. It is here, possibly, that the child meets the unique type of adult-precipitated failure which is in full view of his peers. Failure in school, for many children, represents a goodly portion of the cause for an open break with the adult world. For the majority of inner-city children, failure in the school is a traumatic experience, easily relieved at the permissible age for dropping out of school (Sexton, 1961).

Eliminate Failure

Obviously, an immediate consequence of the preceding is the fact that failure should be eliminated whenever possible from the student's universe, or at least within the purview of the school. This can be accomplished in many ways, some of which are as follows: Arrange classroom activities so there is ample room for a range of topics. Encourage students to stay within the compass of their ability, offering the possible as well as the probable. Have some easy-to-do assignments available so that the child can have success in your class. These assignments can be as simple as erasing the board or taking roll. Many children go through the school day without one instance of success; the inner-city child often suffers this fate through the total day. An interesting challenge is for the teacher to find at least one task for each student that will result in success. Where possible, avoid situations which are too difficult. Always avoid negative criticism by giving continuing support, even if of varying degrees. In many cases, the stolid *good* serves the same purpose as lavish praise. Be warm, cheerful, patient, and consistent (Peck, 1960).

There are also mechanical devices which add support to the classroom attempting a "failure-controlled" atmosphere. The multiple track system attempts to group students by ability and interest. Programmed instruction, especially the linear approach, provides individual instruction predicated upon repeated success.

Success vs. Success

Under normal conditions, the teacher is responsible for the students' successes and failures. And to complete the cycle, the students are responsible for the teacher's successes and failures. The situation is purely ecological with the notion of discipline being the tool that each organism may use to destroy the other. Clearly, children from poorer neighborhoods have not had the intellectual and social experiences which should allow them the skills to get along successfully in the adult world. Their failures may emerge through behavior interpreted as cynical, apathetic, and prejudiced. Such behavior confuses the functions and tasks of discipline and often disappoints teachers who react by giving up the teaching function and adopting discipline as their major function (Toby, 1957).

To summarize to this point, while discipline is both a function and a task of the school, the concept "discipline" may differ to both the teacher from the middle class and the student from the lower class. To the teacher, discipline may be good and self-imposed (as in the aphorism: "I could hardly keep from laughing"), while to the student, discipline is the proof that adults do not understand him. The suggestion made here is that removal of unnecessary failure from both the child's sphere of life and that of his teacher is the common denominator for both concepts of discipline.

Adjust Standards

In order for the reader to accept this common denominator, he might have to adjust some arbitrary standards. The standards may be social as well as educational, but primarily they are arbitrary. If the school is to succeed, it must prevent any reification of the concept that it is a "failure producer." This is not to say that the inner-city child will always require some level of support, but rather that this is an approach to getting started. Too often the new teacher is immobilized by the presence of the inner-city child and waits helplessly for a miracle to happen—some *deus ex machina*. A total support approach, although not easy, is a beginning and provides the teacher with a way of life in the classroom. This suggestion of organizing the classroom curriculum to meet fully the needs of a "failure-shy" child can be justified by alerting the reader to the fact that inner-city children, with their deep sense of inadequacy, are expert in the art of making the unsophisticated teacher feel and act as if he were totally incompetent. A result of this occurrence is usually the loss of a potentially good teacher from the inner-city schools. Being prepared, and forewarned, is an aid toward doing a good job, but actively pursuing a goal, such as a comfortable classroom milieu, is a positive step toward doing an excellent job. The reward for such an accomplishment will be to see your own as well as the student's self-assurance grow. Perhaps the most astounding fact is that, in the vast majority of cases, the mere understanding of this child's need for success, and subsequent acceptance of some non-middle-class habits, are all that may be required to reduce the gap between teacher and student (Combs, 1962).

Defining the Task

For the purpose of examining some classroom situations, the following definitions of education are made:

(1) Education is the process whereby the student becomes independent of the teacher.
(2) The purpose of gathering students together is to use their time in controlled pursuits of education.
(3) Discipline is both function and task to control the pursuits of one or many students.

Controlled pursuits manifest themselves in different ways. In industrial arts, for example, students may be attempting the same group project, each progressing at his individual rate, each completing an item that is the same, yet different from the others. In mathematics, however, every student may be asked to focus upon a specific problem, from a specific page, at a specific moment. There is no one approach that is peculiar to any particular subject area, and most classroom sessions consist of a combination. Many teachers are cautious of experimenting with different approaches for fear that the class will become difficult to control. For example, forming the class into six different teams may result in a six-fold increase in the effort of classroom control. Very often through experimentation, however, a teacher will develop a technique which aids immeasurably in controlling the class, thereby allowing greater freedom to both teacher and student.

For example, Mrs. B. was an auditorium teacher in a junior high school. As part of the semester's work, the students were to present group reports. During the periods allotted for the preparation of the reports, the various small groups were scattered throughout the auditorium in what would have seemed as a ward in *Bedlam* to the casual observer. Whenever Mrs. B wanted silence, she merely played a certain chord on the piano, and a seemingly rowdy class became well-behaved.

Many teachers rely upon some predetermined signal with which to alert the class that they are to come to attention. Some use a tapping of a piece of chalk, a clearing of the throat, or even a loud, "Quiet!" The important ingredients, however, are that there is reason for the signal and the signal remains constant. In the case of Mrs. B., on the very first day of class she informed her students the chord would mean for them to be quiet and attentive. Also, the chord was used to quiet them prior to the end of the period each day, and was integrated into the routine of group presentations and announcements. In a very short period of time, the response (quiet) to the conditioned stimulus (chord) was second nature to the class. By retaining the signal for two teachers sharing the auditorium, all the students were aware of the request made by the chord. Even those students new to the building were made aware of the powerful sound by the quiet response of those around them. *Children do want to know the rules of the game, and there is usually no complaint when these rules are consistent.*

Of course, many teachers do more with their class than teach them to respond to a signal. They "sell" themselves by being fair and by constructing a warm and friendly (failure-controlled) atmosphere. They concentrate on those attributes which students see and hear and often adjust their voice, manner, and appearance in light of their particular school situation. They add an important dimension to the establishment of good classroom rapport by allowing, whenever possible, their students to set their own goals. For example, students who want to do something different are encouraged. Counseling and guidance techniques are used to guide the rebellious student to seek other projects; the emphasis remains upon not embarrassing the student but having alternative actions available. Students soon discover that they can set and achieve various goals, and many teachers are astute enough to include self-discipline as one of these goals. In this instance, discipline is included as part of the curriculum whereas setting aside time each day for a discussion as to why "we must behave" might never make the point.

Levels of Aspiration

Encouraging individual goals is a more sophisticated step toward expert teaching. For many inner-city children their prior classroom experience may tend to inhibit academic and vocational aspirations. Most students are anxious to tackle a higher goal *if* they have some assurance that they might succeed. With success, even minute success, higher goals are usually considered. On the other hand, failure ordinarily lowers the level of aspiration; but failure need not be viewed as negative and the child can learn that failure may even be a degree of success. Of course, if the goal is some understanding of the need for discipline, then this too may be viewed in the same manner. Give children an opportunity to see where classroom control will take them. For example, walking to the lunchroom may not be a solid success, but point out those times of proper control and give due praise. And waiting outside the building in 60° weather during a fire drill may not be done according to the book, but it *was* better than last time. Allow the goal of controlled pursuits to be realistic and strive toward having the student eventually set them himself. This will tend to make the student independent of the teacher (a defined goal of education) as he realizes that he is able to manage himself (Henderson, 1962).

If Chaos Prevails

Note that the discussion to this point has been emphasizing the preparation of the classroom as opposed to "what to do when the roof falls in." This is because no one has been able to predict just what an upset child will do under the pressure of the many stresses of school life. It may be trite to mention "an ounce of prevention . . . ," but to the classroom teacher faced with the prospect of *not* controlling his students, and it is precisely this which drives the teacher away from teaching, this adage becomes sound advice. To set up a wholesome climate in your room, to be seeking better ways of encouraging your students to "chance it" without fear of failure or reprisal, to be able to turn your back on the class, both figuratively and literally speaking, are only pieces of evidence demonstrating that discipline is merely a by-product of efficient classroom management. Once the students know you, and in turn tell other students, your reputation is fairly well set. Effective teaching does not allow any room for many disciplinary problems.

On the other hand, what about those instances where there is trouble in the classroom. Suppose when Mrs. B., mentioned earlier, struck that chord a student rebelled. Then what? Even without a good cause, there is some cause for this kind of action. Try to be clinical in your analysis of misbehavior. It may be connected with the class, the school, the day, the outside world, or just plain "there." In any case, a good suggestion is to seek the cause(s). By doing this, an element of consistency will be established which will, in the long run, provide standards and very likely solve some problems. And the clinical approach implies a cool head; it is the teacher who blows his top at the slightest provocation who is fair game to the hostile child.

There are no absolutes available for this situation, but some rules of thumb are as follows: Do not provide an audience to the child throwing a tantrum, and do not stand before the class and bicker with the student. Coming from a different world, you will soon find that it is you against their world when involved in a "You did too!"— "I did not!" argument. Learn to be tolerant and understanding of the child's behavior. Many of the actions about him during the hours outside of the classroom are those that teachers know little about.

When you criticize some action, be certain that you are not criticizing his parents or best friend at the same time. If education is to make the student independent of you (as defined here), let him learn to judge what he wants. Do not back the child, or the class, against an immovable wall, but rather allow some room to maneuver. And above all, misbehavior *should not* be taken as a personal affront against the school, or you, its representative. The odds are that if you assume that you will not have any difficulty, then you probably will not.

Evaluate Your Actions

One method of scrutinizing students involved in disciplinary problems is to set up a scale upon which the determinants of school incidents can be evaluated. This instrument should offer some system of rating so that both the student's actions and the teacher's may be followed as they develop in a positive or negative manner. A major purpose of the scale is to offer the teacher a grid upon which student actions can be examined. By constantly referring to this scale, it is possible to evaluate a student's emotional growth. But in a similar manner it would behoove the teacher to develop another scale upon which his reactions to school incidents can be evaluated. Then he too will be able to observe his own growth. As an aid to formulating the teacher's personal scale, an illustrative form is included here with the recommendation that the reader complete it in light of his present beliefs. One word of caution: use pencil and be prepared to make adjustments as the place of discipline within the teaching function becomes more discernible. (See p. 142.)

Summary

The role of the inner-city schools is heightened by the fact that very often it serves as the meeting ground for two different cultures —the teacher's and the child's. The place of discipline in the inner-city school is confused by the fact that it is both function and task, and yet is viewed by some teachers as the worst of tasks, and by others as a mere function of the teaching operation. The cause for this is primarily the misunderstanding of the child by the teacher.

REACTIONS TO DISCIPLINARY PROBLEMS

INCIDENTS	REACTIONS (Check response(s) to each incident)						
	Sarcasm & Ridicule	Involved Administra-tion	Punished Whole Class	Lost Temper	Maintained Composure		
Fighting							
Swearing							
Disruption of Class							
Cheating							
Stealing							

Many children from poor neighborhoods appear sullen to their teachers. For some children, manifestations of this behavior require special attention. For many, however, this is the standard way they relate to the adult world. If the child's classroom is an adult world, as often it becomes through interaction styles some teachers employ, certain children will revert to sullen behavior.

Outside the classroom, poverty's children live in a world of "remote" adults. There is not, for example, the consistency between adult males and females relative to their roles in relation to the child, particularly roles the child can build upon. Additionally, other adults in the community remain silent and remote to the extent the child experiences a sense of anonymity. No one cares much what he does, how he does it, or when it is to be done. He is not the center of adult concern.

In the classroom, the child is placed in a "closed" universe with an adult who is hired to educate him. Moreover, social distance is easily felt by both of these people, the advantaged and the disadvantaged. With the classroom teacher having a definite advantage, not only socially but legally, the child tends to develop ways of altering social distance. In some instances, teacher and child will find it convenient to widen the gap and, consequently, "respect" each other's position. On the other hand, sometimes both the child and teacher together strive to reduce the gap and, although feeling awkward at times, do manage to improve their social positions in respect to each other. Curiously enough, however, child and teacher at best find it difficult to develop anything more than a mechanical kind of social relationship. A child, moreover, to win approval may become overly accommodating and obsequious. This not only tampers with his own self-respect, but can be very upsetting to other members of the class. Additionally, members of the class have ways of employing tactics which encourage self-depreciation of those children who even momentarily may wish to rise above their social handicap. This manifests itself particularly in the area of aspiration. Group performance may influence the individual even in areas where he has no previous experience, and he, in turn, evaluates his chances in reference to the group with which he identifies.

It is, then, a strange situation in which many teachers, new to the inner city, find themselves. As an approach to some sort of action, the suggestion is made to create a comfortable failure-free atmosphere in the classroom. In this way the hope is that cause for disciplinary problems will tend to diminish as the child's behavior indicates that he finds himself capable of succeeding within realistic limits. Many successful teachers adopt this role of total support by arranging the curriculum and all phases of interaction so that the student maintains a semblance of self-respect as he finds continued success.

A further extension is to encourage individual goals to be set by the child, with the aim being growth toward, as phrased by Earl C. Kelley, "The Fully Functioning Self" (1962, pp. 9-20). As part of these goals, the concept of self-discipline should be encouraged by treating it as part of the curriculum, i.e., that which is to be learned. The teacher can accomplish this by assuming the student does want to do better and, in turn, making the student aware of each improvement.

The recommendation, then, is to avoid making discipline the goal in teaching but rather to seek out ways by which the need for discipline is diminished. For those cases where it is too late to prevent problems, the recommendation is to examine the setting in which the action occurred. Candidly speaking, don't panic. Remember there is always tomorrow at which time all parties will be present. For most, life is difficult, and when compounded in the educational setting, it can become impossible. The teacher must recognize that each child is an individual, not a "group," and as individuals should be treated accordingly.

The concerned teacher, then, will not react to the child's malfunctioning behavior through liberal sentiment or scolding but rather will show more curiosity relative to these problems and act with firm, fair, direct action. Most of these children are beyond being inspired by sweetness or threat of punishment, and respond better to honest appraisal, sincerity, and consistent courses of action.

If the school experiences of the child coming from low-income groups are to act as countervailing forces of poverty, ignorance, and poor social behavior, the role of discipline in the school setting must be clearly understood by all concerned. To what extent discipline becomes a function or task is the major challenge to those teachers and administrators who will work in schools serving the very poor. For herein lies the control that adjusts the climate to which all other responsibilities of the school are exposed.

Gene C. Fusco[*]

Reaching the Parents

The vital importance of the home in shaping the educational attitudes and behavior of the child is generally recognized. What happens or does not happen to the child at home largely determines what kind of pupil he will be in school.

School, after all, occupies a relatively small portion of the total time and attention of the child. Most of his time—his weekends, holidays, summer vacations and, of course, the formative preschool years —are spent under the influence of his home and neighborhood.

In light of the great weight of evidence that the intellectually and culturally restricted home life of socially disadvantaged children places heavy obstacles in their path for succeeding in school, many believe that the inner-city schools should make extraordinary efforts to assist parents in overcoming such obstacles.

---

[*] This chapter was written by Gene C. Fusco in his private capacity, and not as a government official. Viewpoints or opinions in this presentation are his own and do not necessarily represent those of the U.S. Office of Education.

Educational Environment of the Home

As part of the current widespread effort to improve and strengthen the educational opportunities of socially disadvantaged children, the educational environment of disadvantaged, as contrasted with those more privileged, homes has come under increasing scrutiny.

A growing body of research indicates that the disadvantaged child's difficulties in school are tied in with an intellectually impoverished home life (Bernstein, 1961; Deutsch, *et al.*, 1964b; Bloom, *et al.*, 1965). Those investigations point out that a child's cognitive development occurs largely in response to a rich and variable range of intellectual stimulation. The relatively restricted intellectual environment of the socially disadvantaged child results in a more circumscribed range of effective stimulation, as compared with children from more privileged homes.

Disadvantaged homes typically lack the large variety of objects, utensils, toys, pictures, books and other reading matter that serve to stimulate language development and verbal functioning in children. Such children are not spoken to, except with sharp commands; adults spend little time reading with these children, and the example of a reading parent is often absent in such homes.

As a result of growing up in an unstimulating and non-demanding intellectual environment, disadvantaged children are usually overwhelmed by exposure to learning tasks in school that exceed their prevailing level of cognitive readiness. Lacking the necessary background of knowledge and the motivation to succeed in school, preconditions to efficient learning, such children lose confidence in their ability to learn. They become increasingly demoralized in the school setting, and disengage themselves from it, psychologically at first, and then physically, as soon as it is legally permissible for them to do so.

Basically, the socially disadvantaged child, unlike his middle-class counterpart, finds the school setting radically different from the life he has lived at home. Robert Hess has presented a number of preliminary findings which show that whereas middle-class parents instill in their children the concept of school and the teacher as resources for learning, disadvantaged parents formulate a different kind of expectation for their children (Hess and Shipman, 1965).

Hess and his colleagues at the University of Chicago launched a study designed to examine the effects of middle-class and working-class home environments upon the cognitive behavior and motivation of the preschool child.

Drawing upon carefully observed and recorded parent-child interaction situations in a laboratory setting, Hess found that school for the disadvantaged child is defined by his parents primarily in terms of institutional demands—how to avoid trouble with the teacher, how to behave toward her and other students, and how to conform and adapt to its social and disciplinary setting.

As an example of how a middle-class parent prepares her daughter for school, Hess cites the following: "I would remind Portia that she was going to school to learn, that her time was to be spent mostly in classrooms with other children, and that any questions or any problems that she might have she could consult with her teacher for assistance." In contrast, Hess provides the following working-class mother's response to the same situation: "I tell John that it is time to go to school now, that he must know how to behave. The first day at school he should be a good boy and should do just what the teacher tells him to do."

Hess contends that in the disadvantaged family context, the nature of parent-child interaction restricts the number and kind of alternatives for action and thought that are opened to the child. The teaching styles of disadvantaged mothers produce a child who relates to authority rather than to rationale, who, although often compliant, is not reflective in his behavior, and for whom the consequences of an act are largely considered in terms of immediate punishment or reward rather than future effects and long-range goals.

The basic difference that Hess finds between the attempts of middle-class and disadvantaged mothers to teach their children a task which is unfamiliar to them is that the former employs a problem-solving strategy, whereas the latter issues commands and expects a conditioned response from the child.

School-Home Cooperation

The cognitive and motivational handicaps which burden socially disadvantaged children in school result largely from their intellectually restricted home and neighborhood life. What can the inner-city school do to help parents prepare their children for the school experience, and to assist parents to reinforce and support educational efforts made by school staff members in behalf of their children?

Some promising approaches for bringing about a working alliance of parents and teachers as part of a broad-gauged effort to improve the educational opportunities of socially disadvantaged children are set forth in this section under *preschool*, *in-school*, and *out-of-school* activities.

Preschool Activities

It is now widely recognized that disadvantaged children can derive substantial educational benefits by beginning school as early as age three or four. In the absence of such a "head start," large numbers of those children fall further and further behind as they move through grade school, increasing the probability that they will fail in school, and in adult life.

In an elementary school in Detroit, a nursery education program for three- and four-year-olds helps parents to better prepare their children for schooling by actively involving them in the teaching-learning activities. The nursery class meets in the late afternoon every other day in a well-equipped room set aside for that purpose at the school. Each parent of the children enrolled is assigned to five children for the purpose of assisting the teacher by doing routine but necessary chores, such as passing out materials, keeping records, serving refreshments, and related non-instructional activities.

Monthly meetings are held in the evening at the school during which the teacher briefly and informally discusses some aspect of early child growth and development. The discussion topics are usually based on questions or observations from the parents. During the meetings, the teacher often describes parent-child activities which may be carried on in the home, such as teaching children to count, reading them nursery rhymes and stories, and helping them discriminate among shapes, weights, colors, and sounds.

At the meetings the teacher encourages the parents to share with the other parents personal accounts of carrying on the activities with their children. The parents generally derive encouragement and support from such exchanges. As a follow-up to the meetings, the teacher visits the homes of her pupils on a regular basis, and often demonstrates at home those practices she has recommended at the monthly meetings.

The director of the nursery school program observed:

> We can now look back on four years of shifting our emphasis in attempts to improve our approaches to both children and parents. In checking on the progress of all children in primary grades, we have evidence that the social adjustment and the academic achievement of children who have benefited from the nursery school experience we provide is markedly superior to that of children who have not had an opportunity to participate in the program.

The director cited some by-products of parent involvement in the nursery school program, including heightened parent interest and increased participation in parent-teacher groups, improved parent attendance at school-sponsored functions, and development of more positive parent attitudes toward professional school personnel.

Some schools in Baltimore involve parents as active observers and interpreters of the learning process in regularly scheduled classes in which their children are enrolled. The parent education unit of the Division of Adult Education sponsors and directs early childhood education programs for children ages two to four. The classes, which meet for two and one-half hours one morning each week for a thirty-week period, were established primarily to help parents prepare their children for the formal schooling experience. Children may not attend classes without their parents, although parents and other adults may attend without children.

During the classroom sessions, parents observe the various activities involving the children and record their reactions on a form containing questions intended to guide their observations, e.g., "How did a child make friends?" "How did the teacher encourage children to participate in the painting group?"

In the final hour of the two and one-half hour session, while an assistant teacher supervises the children, the parents assemble in an adjoining room to discuss some of their problems in child rearing with the professional nursery school teacher.

Throughout the program, parents keep written records of their children's home learning activities on a form which, like the form mentioned earlier, contains guiding questions. The teacher reads the written records each week, writes comments on them, and returns them to the parents. These annotated records, along with the teacher's evaluation of the child's development in class, serve as a basis for individual parent-teacher conferences which are scheduled, as needed, during the program. These conferences explore the progress of both the child and his parent in the nursery school program.

After participating in the program for ten weeks, one mother of four small children, two of whom attended the classes, observed that she no longer felt overwhelmed by her responsibilities at home. "I have a much better understanding of why the children behave as they do and I am now better able to handle situations which I did not know how to cope with before attending the nursery school program. I have also acquired a better understanding of why I react as I do to certain situations involving the children at home."

The nature and purpose of the parent-observation classes prompted the supervisor of parent education in the Baltimore school system to refer to the program as "practice teaching in parenthood." She observed: "Our expectation is that seeing-and-doing activities, reinforced by meaningful discussions with other parents faced with similar child-rearing tasks, are more likely to influence the parents' daily home learning activities with their children than simply listening to someone tell them how to do it. Then too, the nursery school experience conditions parents to work closely with the teacher, to trust her and confide in her, to respect her professional judgment and skill. Such parents typically become firm allies of the school."

In an elementary school in Baltimore, a series of meetings are set up in the spring for the purpose of helping parents better prepare their children for school. Parents of children entering in the fall are contacted through personal visits by teachers early in the spring and told about the series. At the initial meeting, parents are given a preview of the series.

The meetings are planned by a committee of classroom teachers, the school nurse, the home visitor, and social worker from the central office who are assigned to the school. Under the guidance of the principal, assignments for brief presentations which are followed by small group discussions, are cooperatively developed. At the meetings, teachers and others call attention to child developmental tasks and offer parents practical suggestions for promoting child activities at home designed to broaden and enrich their educational environment.

The social worker and home visitor inform the parents about their responsibilities in the school, about ways in which they can help parents directly, and also about community resources, especially recreational and health facilities located in the nearby neighborhood. At the final meeting of the series, children in the first-grade class present a program for the parents which highlights some of the classroom activities they engaged in when they were in kindergarten. That program includes a tour of the school; kindergarten facilities and the play area are given special emphasis.

"One of the greatest obstacles we have to overcome in enlisting parent participation in our school," observed the school principal, "is the fact that they are fearful and suspicious of the school setting —and of us. Many have had unhappy school experiences themselves and they communicate their hostility to their children. We believe this series of spring meetings helps them, especially when reinforced with appropriate summer followup activities."

The principal pointed out that several avenues are used to inform parents of the spring meetings. For example, notices about meetings are left with local ministers to announce during Sunday service. In addition, members of the room mothers' organization serve as volunteers to inform other parents of the meetings. They contact a certain number of parents who, in turn, agree to contact a given number, and so on. Children are asked to urge their parents to attend the meetings, and notices are sent home periodically.

In several schools in Philadelphia, school-home coordinators interpret the school program to parents and provide teachers with information about home conditions that may help them become more effective in improving the academic status and behavior of individual pupils. The coordinators, responsible to the building principal, are lay persons carefully selected on the basis of their leadership qualities and the high status they enjoy among their neighbors. In the spring, the coordinators make periodic visits to the homes of such families, and assist the parents to help their children sucessfully make the transition from home to school.

During their first visit, coordinators carry a leaflet produced by the school system which contains general information about the school schedule, program, and services. In cases where parents are illiterate or semi-literate, the coordinator explains and interprets the contents of the leaflet to them. During the course of their visits, coordinators encourage parents to buy popular magazines and discuss the pictures contained in them with their children. They also encourage parents to read their children appropriate stories, to play simple games with them, and to talk to their children about current events and everyday happenings.

The coordinators urge parents in need of such services to attend literacy classes and to enroll in other adult education programs operated by the Adult Education Division of the Philadelphia school system. In addition, the coordinators encourage parents to participate in parent-teacher groups and to visit the school to meet the professional staff on pre-registration day in late spring.

One of the coordinators, a long-time resident of the neighborhood, and a mother of five children herself, reviewed her contacts with parents during the past year. "My approach with both mothers and fathers is direct and simple, and sometimes, blunt. I try to help them to understand that the school people work hard to help their children succeed academically, but that they cannot do that job alone. I tell them that they owe it to their children to cooperate with the school." She added, "Those parents know me. They know that I am their friend and that I—and the school teachers—share a common concern: to improve the education and welfare of their children."

In-School Activities

Many culturally disadvantaged parents have had a limited education, are semi- or unskilled laborers, and are barely literate. They are self-conscious about their attire, speech patterns, and undeveloped social skills. As a result, they are often reluctant to visit the school and associate an invitation for a conference with a member of the school staff as a summons for discussion of their child's behavioral or academic difficulties. Typically, such parents are highly reluctant to intervene with school authorities in behalf of their children, and are often suspicious, and even hostile, toward school personnel.

In an elementary school in Detroit, a "special class contract" binds the parents to work closely with the teacher in behalf of their child. A teacher-parent conference is arranged when a teacher determines that remedial instruction for a school child is needed. The principal sends the parents a notice informing them that their child would benefit from remedial classes, which are held twice each week after regular school hours. The bottom half of the notice lists alternate hours and days of the week for an appointment with the teacher.

If the parents consent to have their child participate in the program, the teacher arranges for a conference, at which time she explains the purpose of the "Special Class Contract." According to the contract, the parents agree that if the child is accepted in the special class, they will make certain that their child attends regularly. Parents must also agree, according to the contract, "To help my child at home as asked by the teacher." The contract concludes, "I understand that if I do not fulfill the above agreement, my child will be dropped from the class."

During the parent-teacher conferences, which are scheduled on a regular basis for the duration of the remedial instruction program, parents are encouraged to: (1) read daily to their child; (2) listen to their child read; (3) ensure that the child has pencils, paper, a notebook, and a dictionary for home study; and (4) provide a quiet, well-lighted study area in the home for study and reading. Parents are constantly reminded that if they show that they value school achievement, their child will likewise value it.

The assistant principal commented that the arrangement elicits from the parents a commitment to cooperate with the school in behalf of their child. "Parents often have to be convinced of our sincerity to help their child succeed in school. They respond positively and enthusiastically to our suggestions for helping their child succeed in school. These suggestions are communicated to them through our regularly scheduled teacher-parent conferences. We find that the natural desire of parents to do the best they can for their child sustains the contract agreement."

Group conferences by grade level are held by teachers in an elementary school in Chicago to familiarize parents with ways in which they can reinforce school activities involving their children. Parents are contacted through home visits, or by first-class mail. Follow-up contact is made to verify that parents will attend an informal conference at which the principal, teachers, and pupil personnel workers inform parents about how the home can reinforce school activities. At these meetings volunteers greet people at the door, pin name tags on them, and serve refreshments. These conferences also serve as a means of inviting parents to sign up for individual conferences with teachers.

The parent education consultant serving the school observed that the parent-teacher conferences "are as useful to the professional staff as they are to the parents. It is imperative for us to know about parent attitudes toward their children's schooling and to learn about home conditions that affect a child's learning and behavior. The more we know, the more we can help the parents."

During the group conferences, parents are encouraged to hold extended conversations with their children. They are urged to ask their children such questions as "What did you play outside?" "What happened at kindergarten today?" "Tell me about the children you played with today." Further, parents are encouraged to stimulate self-expression in their children by asking them a series of questions as they look at pictures in popular magazines. Parents are also urged to count objects with their children, to help them to write their name, and discriminate between colors and sounds. Parents are reminded at the conferences that the school staff is always happy to see them to answer questions "about what your child is doing in school or why we are doing what he tells you."

A series of parent information and discussion group sessions involving parents of seventh-grade pupils is conducted at a junior high school in Detroit. Parents are contacted by school-community agents who set up the sessions in cooperation with classroom teachers. Two group sessions are conducted to reach as large a number of parents as possible, one in the early afternoon and another in the evening. A given class session is held twice each week for a four-week period.

In addition to informing parents about the school program and services, and about ways that parents can help their children prepare for high school, parents are encouraged to raise questions about any aspect of adolescent behavior which they find difficult to understand. Pupil personnel workers are brought in to assist in the discussions.

One of the school-community agents commented, "We felt that we tapped a vital parent need in setting up this series. We discovered that 90 per cent of the parents who participated were not involved in other parent activities sponsored by the school." The agent called attention to the enthusiasm of parents who took advantage of the opportunity to participate in the discussion groups. "They liked the small, permissive classes," he observed, and pointed out that the parents who participated in the sessions told others about them, and attendance at the second series increased markedly.

A parent discussion class is also held at the high school which receives graduates from the junior high school mentioned above. A school-community agent commented that plans are underway to establish a similar discussion group in a feeder elementary school. "In that way," he added, "we can have an unbroken line of parent-orientation classes from elementary through high school."

An intensive effort is made by a school social worker attached to a school in Baltimore to reach a group of "unreachable" parents. The social worker assigned to an elementary school in Baltimore described her deep concern about unfavorable family conditions that adversely affected children's intellectual and social development in school. "I found through home visits that children referred to me by teachers because of deviant behavior in school were often illegally absent from school, hungry, untidy, and ill-clothed. They disliked school intensely." She added, "In my attempt to involve some of their parents in helping them to assume greater responsibility for their child's school adjustment, I found these homes did not provide the kinds of experiences which could serve as a bridge to the school setting. The parents really wanted to cooperate with the school in the education of their children, but they didn't know how to go about it."

The social worker enlisted the aid of the Adult Education Department to provide appropriate guidance and assistance to a selected group of ten parents whose children were having academic difficulty and behavior problems. The social worker pointed out that though the adult education unit normally does not provide an instructor for fewer than fifteen parents, the smaller group could be justified because the enrollees were parents of large families totaling 40 children, including preschoolers.

The class met weekly for one and one-half hours in the afternoon, for a four-month period, under the guidance of a discussion leader supplied by the Adult Education Department, who worked closely with the social worker. Discussion topics covered a wide spectrum of interests and needs, including organization of household tasks, meal planning and nutrition, clothing construction, managing a budget, filling in job application forms, and the various ways that parents could help their children succeed in school.

The social worker checked periodically with the teachers and at the end of the program was able to report that the physical appearance of both parents and children improved, as did the children's behavior and motivation to learn. "This is a two-way street," she observed. "The teachers have to learn too and adjust their own perceptions to the realities of parent readiness to undertake an active role in supporting school efforts made on behalf of their children."

In a series of meetings with teachers, held during the same period as the parent meeting, the social worker attempted to provide them with some insights regarding the underlying causes for certain parent behavior patterns. "I tried to help the teachers recognize that parent apathy, and even hostility toward school served as self-protection against what appeared to them to be rejection from still another institution, representing to them authority and coercion."

The social worker told the following vignette in connection with the group of parents with whom she worked: "Mrs. M., the mother of eight school-age children, was urged by the social worker to enroll in the class to benefit her children, who regularly came to school tardy, whose attendance was poor, and whose academic achievement was low. After the fifth session, the mother's own personal appearance improved. Gradually, desirable changes in the children became evident. They began to come to school on time and regularly, and subsequently their behavior became less erratic. Then the mother took an increased interest in their progress report, and she subsequently attended parent-teacher meetings with her husband. By the end of the school year, we noted a significant improvement in physical appearance, health, and academic achievement of the children."

Out-of-School Activities

Disadvantaged parents often do not provide their children with a broad range of intellectually stimulating opportunities outside the home and neighborhood, opportunities which more privileged parents provide their children at an early age. The disadvantaged adult seldom emerges from his neighborhood confinement. He is often psychologically and physically restricted to its circumscribed area.

At a junior high school in Philadelphia, excursions to a variety of places are planned, conducted, and evaluated with the cooperation of the parents. Working together with school-community coordinators, parents play an important part in planning Saturday bus trips. Visits are made to places of historical interest, museums of art and science, industrial plants, food distribution centers, airports, parks, farms, housing developments, and libraries. At planning sessions before the trip, parents are told about what to expect while in transit and at the destination. The principal of the school observed: "We wanted the parents to participate, to feel a part of what was going on, and to actively share the experience with their children. We didn't want them to serve as glorified babysitters."

The school-community coordinator noted that parents seek information about proper dress, about procedures in ordering from a menu and tipping in a restaurant, and ask for guidance on a variety of social situations unfamiliar to them. The coordinator commented that the bus trips offer some parents the first opportunity they have ever had to eat a meal in a restaurant with their families. Parents are encouraged to attend museums and libraries in the city with their children. "Most of them didn't know that there was no fee required to attend public places, such as museums," observed the principal. "Before the trip, they were uneasy about their attire, about saying something inappropriate. But after the initial experience, and the satisfactions derived from it, they were eager to visit another place of interest. Before long, they were making family trips to the city on their own."

In addition, parents are sent a weekly flyer entitled "Enrichment Opportunities for You and Your Children" which includes a list of suggested places to visit in the city for enrichment purposes. The flyer names cultural, educational, and recreational facilities available to the public. Parents are encouraged to broaden and enrich their experiential backgrounds by joining the children on trips to the places listed in the flyers.

At an elementary school in Chicago, a booklet entitled "Neighborhood Aids" was prepared for parents by the Community Relations Committee of the School Staff. The booklet lists the names and addresses of health services, social service agencies, legal assistance agencies, nursery schools, counseling services, and recreational and cultural agencies in the larger community.

A committee from the school staff also prepared a booklet for parents of academically talented students. Entitled "Interesting Places to Visit in Chicago," it lists cultural centers which can provide the students and parents with opportunities to enrich their knowledge and experiences. The booklet lists libraries, guided tours, museums, conservatories, zoos, recreational facilities, and exhibits available to the public.

The booklets are presented to parents in connection with evening Parent Teacher Association meetings. The nature and purpose of the booklets are explained by teachers. Follow-up visits to the homes are made by teachers to reinforce and supplement the information contained in the booklets.

One of the teachers who served on the committee that drafted the booklet commented: "On the basis of comments and questions from the parents following trips to public places suggested by the booklets, we believe our efforts have been highly worthwhile." She also observed that semi-literate or illiterate parents are identified through home visits by social workers and special efforts are made to communicate the information to them, and to encourage them to enroll in literacy classes at school.

A parent survey made by a committee of teachers in an elementary school in Baltimore revealed cultural deficits which the school attempted to remedy. Information gathered by the teachers concerning the cultural pursuits of parents in the neighborhood was analyzed and distributed to the faculty.

The questionnaire survey had yielded the information that 90 per cent of the families had television sets and watched programs regularly. This information led the committee to compile a list of programs of educational value to parents and their children. These lists were distributed to the homes through the children. The potential benefits of certain TV programs were underscored at meetings of the Parent Teacher Association and at meetings of room mother clubs.

During monthly meetings of room mother clubs, teachers informed parents of ways in which they could enlarge their children's experiences. For example, mothers were shown how the daily newspaper could be used as a source of information about current events and local cultural activities in the city.

In addition, bus trips on weekends were organized by the school, enabling parents and children to attend concerts, ballets, and plays together. Each trip was followed up by appropriate activities in the classroom and by an appraisal of the trip at Parent Teacher Association meetings. Parents were also taken to a local public library, shown how to use the reference file, and encouraged to use the library frequently.

At an elementary school in Detroit, the school-community agent works with both teachers and parents in planning, conducting, and assessing pupil-parent field trips. The school-community agent works with parents weeks in advance of the scheduled bus trips. The time is spent in helping parents budget their money in order to save enough for the trip, assisting them in planning lunches where appropriate, and in preparing them for activities which are new to them, such as dining in a restaurant or visiting a zoo. The school-community agent holds both pre-trip and post-trip meetings with parents. Those meetings provide her with opportunities to determine parent needs and responses to the experience, which aid her in scheduling future trips.

The trips to the city and surrounding area have included tours by boat and train, and a walk along a nature trail. Trips have also been made to nearby colleges and high schools and to farms, local industries, business establishments, radio stations, museums, parks, and transportation terminals. Commenting on the values which parents derive from such trips, a school-community agent said, "The trips broaden the cultural horizon of parents, and whet their appetites for more experiences. We encourage them to make such excursions on their own after guiding them on one or two trips. Typically, they take their children with them, and adult and child learn together."

On Teacher Perceptions of Parents

A general principle which I believe may be derived from the school-home practices described above is: *Generally, socially disadvantaged parents are interested in their children's education and are eager for them to succeed in school; their seeming indifference and apathy reflect their lack of knowledge regarding the nature of the demands the school will place on their children, and their lack of skills concerning ways in which they can prepare their children for the transition from home to school, and reinforce and support school efforts made on behalf of their children.*

If this view is correct, it is evident that the inner-city school must take the initiative in bridging the gap between school and home. The prime responsibility for launching such efforts lies with the school principal, who can define the problem to his staff and develop the necessary administrative organization to facilitate staff efforts to assist parents in helping their children succeed in school.

But even a combination of administrative ingenuity, generous financial support, appropriate facilities, and pupil personnel services provided by the central office is not enough to tip the scales toward improved school-home cooperation in depressed neighborhoods. Concerned and dedicated teachers, sensitive to the need for reaching parents, and willing to extend themselves in terms of time, energy, and creative effort are essential to the achievement of that purpose.

Indeed, a thread running through the practices described in this chapter is that the cooperative relationships between parent and teacher developed through face-to-face contacts are a key factor in improving school-home ties. As the person who has close and regular contact with pupils, the classroom teacher is the key agent for establishing and maintaining close working relations with parents. She carries out this responsibility by making home visits, by conducting individual and group conferences with parents at school, by maintaining a working alliance with pupil personnel workers, and by any other means that will give her sharper insights into home conditions that influence the learning and behavior of children in her charge.

In considering the imperative need for effective communication between the middle-class oriented teacher and the socially disadvantaged parent, the burden of initiating contact, exploring avenues of mutual interest, and maintaining effective interaction lies with the teacher. The dynamics of such relationships may best be considered in terms of an important and growing movement in psychological thought—variously called the perceptual, interactional, or existential approach to understanding man's behavior.

The perceptual view of human behavior holds that the behavior of an individual is a function of his ways of perceiving. That is to say, how any person behaves at a given moment is a direct expression of the way things seem to him at that moment. A person does not behave according to the "facts" as they seem to an outsider, but rather as a result of how things seem to him in terms of the personal meanings (perceptions) existing for him at the moment of action (Combs, 1962).

Social psychologists and other behavioral scientists call attention to the fact that we humans see and hear what we want to see and hear; that we are remarkably adept at believing what we have never seen—and seeing what we have come to believe.

As Wendell Johnson says, "When we speak about the world as we observe it, and the people in it, we talk largely in terms of our feelings about it and them, or our judgments about it and them." He adds, "We do not *describe* things, persons, and events; we more commonly *evaluate* them as beautiful or good, wise or stupid, ugly or bad. Such words describe nothing. They express our personal standards and reflect our feelings about whatever we may be responding to" (Johnson, 1956, p. 75).

Thus, our descriptions about people are expressive of our inner states—feelings, preconceptions, assumptions, delusions, or hopes. It turns out sometimes, that what we report to ourselves—or others—as factual observations are mainly or purely self-projections. There is, indeed, a measure of self-projection involved in anything we say. And regardless of what else we seem to be talking about, Johnson points out, we always, in some degree, are talking about ourselves.

For the classroom teacher who attempts to improve and strengthen relations with socially disadvantaged parents, the admonition, "what we look at is not what we see," should serve as a constant reminder of the pitfalls in her path. What the teacher sees when she is in personal contact with a disadvantaged parent is determined only partly by what stares her in the face. Does she see beyond the halting words, awkward mannerisms, downcast eyes, ill-fitting clothing? What the teacher sees is shaped by her wishes and doubts, likes and dislikes, her fears, assumptions, knowledge and ignorance.

Thus, when teachers and other school personnel make an unwarranted evaluation ("Mrs. B. is lazy," or "apathetic," or "disinterested in her children's education"), there is little likelihood that they will explore avenues for improving communication with Mrs. B. Indeed, such an appraisal may bring about a self-fulfilling prophecy—Mrs. B. may behave in such a way as to conform to the behavior expected of her. On the other hand, when school personnel assess people and situations in descriptive terms ("Mrs. B. does not attend school-sponsored functions," or "did not respond to our invitation for a conference about her child"), then they are more likely to attempt to identify the causes for Mrs. B's behavior, which could well lead them to re-examine their approaches for reaching the parents. Until now, reaching the parents was a desirable goal; henceforth it will be a necessity.

Robert D. Strom

Summary

Importance of the Inner-City Teacher

The job function a teacher assumes and the manner in which its tasks are performed depend upon how important one perceives his position to be. Clearly there is little promise for students with those who admit to being jailors rather than guides, who consider their charge one of keeping youth out of trouble instead of improving minds. Neither can development be the theme in classrooms where educators are frustrated and disappointed by the chasm between the role they hoped for and what their immediate situation seems to present. Yet, Niemeyer suggests these views are held by a large, though indeterminate, number of inner-city teachers. And, though they differ in method for coping with the assignment by transfer, quitting, waiting for retirement, or resigning themselves to a career of inefficiency and martyrdom—there is agreement that the job is really not very important. Others feel that the role could be significant were it not for the fact that students' homes tend to neutralize school influence. As the school apparently cannot change the family, and since the home background precludes educating the child, some teachers, in despair, come to the conclusion that the pupils are unteachable. If teachers feel the role is unimportant, then how important can the role really be? To reverse the negative persuasion there first must be changes in the school designed to overcome this sense of helplessness and frustration which many teachers feel.

If the school is to adapt, as it must, boards of education need to do more than merely confirm the necessity for change. Niemeyer deplores the administrative practice of establishing training institutes for teachers, urging the staff to innovate, and then withdrawing the essential mechanisms for supporting any real change. In certain cases, programs are de-emphasized once the vocal element of the community which called for an updated approach is assured their request has been initiated. Very often a visit to schools six months after introduction of a new emphasis indicates that teachers have reverted back to the old methods due to lack of promised materials, inadequate supervision to turn to for help when difficulties arise with new techniques, complaints by those in authority of unacceptable noise, or pressure from colleagues to sustain tradition.

Apart from more substantial administrative backing, teachers can enhance their role by an improved understanding of the pupil audience whom they serve and how these children can better be reached. The rapid rate of intellectual development at life's beginning by which a child gains as much of his mature intelligence in the first four years (50 per cent) as during the next thirteen years which follow (50 per cent), has lead a number of writers to assume our only chance with disadvantaged students is during the early years. However, lest we put all our effort into one alternative, Niemeyer reports findings from the New York Demonstration Guidance Project which indicate that even in junior high school appreciable gains can be made, given the right program. Most of the successful projects have been predicated more on thorough education and attention to special needs of children than on newly discovered techniques. While there is nothing novel about taking pupils on field trips, assessing academic difficulty, or operating remedial programs, these procedures are notably absent in many schools. Further, a number of successful methods for teaching low-income children are known and have been described in books and periodicals. In short, we do not have to wait for the answers as a number of answers already are available.

Niemeyer suggests that important aspects of teacher role are necessarily devaluated when a disproportionate amount of time is spent on matters of discipline. Describing a study in which 80 per cent of class schedule time involved keeping order and findings by other investigators indicating the low-income families' emphasis on being good in school, Niemeyer points to the need for showing children of the poor that education involves more than just behaving, more than physical conformity—its greatest dimension is the learning process. After giving several examples at various grade levels of ways to make lessons more meaningful, the author concludes with a warning that "to continue the educational programs which currently typify the majority of inner-city classrooms is to march irrevocably toward explosive failure."

Teacher Aspiration and Attitude

Whether one will experience frustration or success upon encountering children of the inner city depends a great deal upon his aspirations and attitudes. In our time, emotional logic and social fiction combine to urge a negative view of poverty's children so that although few of us know any of the poor as individuals, it is convenient to think of them all in terms of recalcitrance, resignation, drunkenness, apathy, immorality, and disease. Armed with this frame of reference, many new teachers assigned to neighborhoods of low income can hardly be expected to cherish their task. In fact, many of them will prejudge their class by its environment before ever confronting individual pupils. Strom asserts that the result of determining progress before instruction begins is to render countless boys and girls immobile, children for whom advance will ever be elusive.

Inappropriate academic expectations also portend misfortune for both teacher and pupils. A common course is for the initial goals to be unrealistically high in hopes of motivating members of the class to extricate themselves from the subculture. Then, when students are unable to reach beyond ability and achieve these elevated objectives, instructors tend to exchange extremes in expectation and capitulate to low aims. Teacher inability to revise expectations without abandoning them, to alter the ends without sacrifice to instruction is perhaps the greatest deterrent to effective instruction. With substitution of low goals for lofty ones is the accompaniment of a new emphasis as mental process comes to be replaced by accentuation of physical behaviors—job function changes from instruction to taking care of children with primary attention devoted more to matters of discipline than learning.

Ordinarily the primary source for teacher aspiration is the intelligence test score. That educators might be more reticent in using an intelligence quotient as a comprehensive index of mental functioning, Strom reviews data regarding the lack of comparability between ratings obtained under different auspices, the contribution of culture-free measures in eliminating test bias, and the range of abilities assessed by common measures of intellect. In cases where pupil experience has been so deviant as to render an accurate view of potential unlikely by using standard assessment, it is advisable to supplement with tests of other mental functions. We err in structuring curricula and materials to bring out only the kinds of growth considered by tests of IQ for these tests represent only a limited number of functions. It follows they are an inadequate base for determining mental retardation and giftedness, grouping or grading. While intelligence tests will continue to be useful, we ought not to expect more from their findings than the results can offer. Strom believes educators must expand their concept of the human mind so as to allow children to learn in creative ways, to sanction the use of abilities not currently assessed by traditional measures of mental functioning.

That every school activity bears the influence of teacher aspiration and attitude is shown in the juxtaposition of autocratic and democratic classrooms. In the former, learner roles are characterized by an overemphasis on reactivity, listening and reporting teacher-given data in its original form. Experiment, discovery, discussion—these modes of learning are off limits. As few questions are allowed, the student whose inquiry persists is branded as a "troublemaker," a person who would disrespect authority. On the other hand, a teacher of democratic persuasion fosters creativity, encourages questions, consultation, experimentation, and discovery. He does not assume the omniscient or omnipotent role but instead admits to being uninformed on some matters, allows pupil opinion to register change in the class, and maintains different expectations for each youngster.

As impersonality in the school setting relates more to teacher attitude than class size, it is suggested that certain impersonal responses can be reduced apart from a decline in pupil-teacher ratio. Unless we can retain the personal approach, there is danger of losing the enthusiasm by which motivation is transferred to students. Then too, attitudes toward the learning process and its measure show up in the kinds and amount of homework assigned as well as the nature of evaluation chosen. Unless these are reasonable, we induce defeat. In every instance, the conclusion is inescapable—our aspirations and attitudes must favor the progress of all children if the professional commitment is to be fulfilled.

Overcoming Value Differences

The differences separating an inner-city home from the school its children attend are often exaggerated and misconstrued. Havighurst believes these differences, reflected in pupil behavior and perform- ance, can best be viewed as gaps in knowledge, skills, and values. Few parents question the desirability of reducing the gap between teacher and pupil where knowledge and skills are concerned. In fact, this goal is embraced by even the least educated adults who, like most of us, desire that their children be afforded opportunities to surpass parental circumstance in terms of occupational status and income. But while inner-city parents clearly recognize the superi- ority of their child's teacher in assisting the young to become pro- ficient as readers, writers, and mathematicians, concession is less often given to the proposition that school staff members can improve upon the values engendered by the home. As a consequence, the value gap becomes a subject of home-school controversy and some- times open competition between the two institutions.

An unsuccessful approach has been to circumvent the value issue by declaring it off limits, by insisting the school lacks moral justi- fication in attempting to teach middle-class values to members of other socioeconomic groups. Perceiving deprived homes as only culturally different, advocates of this strategy urge that we respect the right of the poor to live as they choose. This would seem to imply that the poor can choose the circumstance in which they live rather than live where they do because they can ill-afford to reside else- where. The life space of most poor people does not correspond to choice; only the myopic observer can view an undesirable environment and believe it to be a reflection of the values held by people who live there—life circumstance and value are not always the same.

Havighurst argues that for schools to be successful all children must be taught the following values: desire for a work career based on skills and knowledge; desire for a stable family life; inhibition of aggressive impulses; rational approach to a problem situation; desire for freedom of self and others; punctuality; orderliness; and conformity to group norms. These values are not exclusive to a particular social class. Instead, they are values of an urban, industrial, democratic society. To envisage the school and home each as fostering a different set of values is not to recognize that parents who have been defeated in attempts to achieve certain goals find it difficult if not impossible to instruct youngsters in achieving these same elusive objectives. Were the school to organize a program for teaching some set of specific values like those enumerated above, we might expect support from a number of families whose willingness to assist children is not always evidenced by a logical behavioral concomitant.

To ensure a more favorable value orientation for the inner-city child, the school must use both its cultures to better advantage. According to Havighurst, the school incorporates an instrumental culture and an expressive culture. In the instrumental culture, composed of the academic skills and knowledge formally stated as educational objectives, one is exposed to procedures which are to advance his prowess as a reader, speller, or mathematician. Thus, participation in the instrumental culture is to reach goals beyond the activity itself such as being promoted, becoming a mechanic or a good citizen. In contrast, the expressive culture consists of those activities in which pupils and teachers engage for the sake of the participation itself rather than for some distant goal. Popular aspects of the expressive culture include playing games at recess, participating in musical events, taking part in festivals, the celebration of holidays, school parties, and physical education

The expressive culture is considered best for teaching values because it sustains less severe and unfair competition, thereby allowing more children to succeed. Unfortunately, some schools have policies which deny participation in the expressive culture unless one first succeeds in the instrumental culture. (For example, one cannot be in the band or play football unless he has a "B" average.) Havighurst replies to this philosophy by citing several studies showing that performance in the instrumental culture is improved by value changes which derive from increased participation in the expressive culture. Then too, low-income parents with little academic background can become involved in the expressive culture without fear of embarrassment. In so doing they can come to provide greater support for the school. Our task is not to invade and conquer value-hostile territory of big city slums but to help clarify values which are confused, then to give incentive and direction by which the values can be achieved.

Fostering Creative Behavior

To foster creative behavior is a goal of many inner-city teachers. Many of their colleagues, however, view the prospect with a sense of apprehension, believing that any latitude for pupils would result in a loss of discipline, a classroom in which chaos and disorder would reign. Still others among the school staff maintain the object to be idealistic, an impossibility with children who are basically apathetic, listless, and irresponsive. That all of these teacher groups might better understand the forces which inhibit creative thinking abilities of students as well as recognize certain ways by which such abilities can be developed is a necessary objective for our time.

Among the environmental factors which most impede creative growth is the excessive attention our culture has attached to success. This orientation is necessarily inimical to achievement as the creative approach to learning sponsors risk taking, the choice of hypotheses, making mistakes and then correcting the errors. And, if being incorrect means one is considered less than worthy, less than acceptable, it follows that a number of children will desist in the method of inquiry; others will withdraw; still another group may express disappointment through hostility and aggression. Torrance suggests that if we choose to encourage constructive behavior, teachers may have to modify their concept of success to permit low-income youngsters to first succeed in ways that are possible to them. This implies the use of familial strengths which are brought to school as opposed to insisting they compete in areas foreign to their background.

Additional impediments to creativity include peer pressures for conformity, negative teacher response to divergency, and a misplaced emphasis on sex roles. Torrance speculates that the decline in creative development at the fourth and seventh grade levels might possibly be explained in the urging for conformity which derives from the need for consensual validation. As original and unusual ideas become the target of peer pressures for conformity, many students are reluctant to behave in certain ways until they are assured of the approval by age mates. Elaborating upon his own studies of disadvantaged children which show the increasing fear to deviate as one advances through the grades, Torrance concludes that many youngsters—sensing their unique ideas might be unacceptable to peers—have ceased to respond in creative ways and are no longer open to new experiences. The matter of peer pressure for conformity is exacerbated in classrooms where teachers expect pupil uniformity in motivation and achievement, where persons who deviate from behavioral norms are pictured as mentally sick, undesirable, and in need of correction. Under these conditions, sameness is fostered, conformity considered a virtue.

Similarly in the home and community, creative advance is threatened by a misplaced emphasis on sex roles which result in boys and girls shutting out various dimensions of awareness. We know that receptivity and sensitivity are judged as being feminine in our culture whereas independence in thinking is considered masculine. We also know that creative behavior includes each of these attributes. In one study among potential dropouts of seventh and eighth grade, it was found that 90 per cent of the girls and 15 per cent of the boys feel the best answer to questions is the one the teacher thinks is right. This seems to indicate that inner-city girls are taught to be over-receptive to authority while boys are more likely to find masculine status in actively rejecting an authority figure like the teacher.

For children to achieve mental potential, teachers should recognize that creative behavior involves the capacity to wonder, to be puzzled, and to respond constructively. These capacities, expressed in the questions of young people, are often dismissed, disregarded, or punished by adults who view the curious child as annoying and threatening. Torrance describes several workshops in which teachers have been taught how to ask provocative questions which call for responses of flexibility, fluency, originality, and elaboration. Teachers in the workshops have also been taught to respond to unusual questions in such a way so as to enable the student to pursue his own answer, retain his curiosity and realize that his instructor respects original contributions. Examples are given of successful methods for helping children become creative readers, and developing powerful skills of inquiry through research tools. In all these techniques, the reference point is the individual. Because this is so, learning is more personal, more satisfying, and more effectual.

Improving the Pupil Self-Concept

There is an integral relationship between self-concept and behavior. For those who think of themselves as inferior, unworthy, or inept, the tendency is to act in ways that are self-defeating even though a variety of approaches to life be chosen. Bowman estimates the tragedy of this course involves over one-half of all inner-city children—boys and girls who hold such a baneful image of themselves as to hinder or prevent academic progress. Unless these children can be helped to achieve dignity during their youth, it is dubious whether they will find constructive roles as adults. To exchange a positive image for the damaged ego they sustain is a monumental task, a societal responsibility which will require something more ennobling than just the provision of better housing and a reduction of physical needs.

For those who would assist the unsuccessful, there is a necessity to recognize some of the ways by which these boys and girls see themselves. Essentially, the self-view seems to be dominated by four main themes: failure, alienation, unfair treatment, and hopelessness. From the cradle these children have been witnesses of failure—they see parents who have been defeated in attempts to obtain a reasonable family income; the kind of house they live in is undesirable; the disrupted home bespeaks a dilution of affection; and street life offers countless examples of men and women who have deserted their ideals. The association with failure becomes personal upon entering elementary school as in the new setting the youngsters find themselves unprepared to meet teacher expectations. Later they are subject to the ridicule and disapproval of peers whose background and attainment exceed their own. In time they come to avoid participation in school activities and desire to leave the institution.

Alienation as a theme originates in the family when its members feel unwanted or see themselves as an economic burden to their parents and siblings. This injury to self-esteem becomes more pronounced when an individual is excluded from peer affiliation by age mates whose acceptance requires his neighborhood, parents, and dress to differ from what they are or can be. Bowman observes that these social barriers do not create a greater cohesion among low-income children. Indeed, girls often are lonely and boys' gangs seem more to be a liaison for mutual support among the rejected than association of close personal ties. Under these conditions, one naturally comes to regard himself as a victim, one whom others are out to get, an individual who is receiving unfair treatment. This attitude is manifest in the judgment slum children offer regarding instruction, for 90 per cent of their criticisms center around mistreatment by teachers. The final negative stage is that of capitulation to despair, apathy, and the belief that the future is not worth preparing for.

Generally the elevation of self-concept for deprived youth has been accomplished by one of several agents. First of these is the parents who can be trained to assist children in helping reach for and attain desirable goals. Adult identification and self-respect can also be achieved when one gets a job and enters the labor market. A good marriage, with responsibilities, can assist an individual in his gain of maturity. Finally, the influence of a significant adult outside the family may be the needed stimulus. What is disheartening to realize is that while middle-class children often remember classroom experiences as a major influence in their lives, such accounts are foreign to the above list of positive influences cited by adolescents of the inner city. Bowman's conclusion: No longer can we allow the self to be developed by chance or some peripheral endeavor within the school. Instead, the dignity of each pupil must become central to institutional purpose as expressed in a comprehensive but individualized academic program which allows all to succeed. In other words, the school must change before we can expect the child to change.

If we are to accomplish our purpose, students must be allowed active partnership in the learning process. The ordinary procedure by which teachers spend 70 to 90 per cent of class time talking while pupils listen should be reversed. Bowman advocates a reduction in the evaluative comments of teachers—not only because these children live in the midst of constant negative judgment but because an adequate self-concept can only be based upon the opportunity for self evaluation. Decision making as a joint venture of teachers and students is also desirable. Unless these kinds of shift occur in the locus of authority and control, there is much less chance that "pupils will be allowed to participate actively, learn from their own mistakes, develop interest in what they are doing—and these are the roads to positive change in self-concept."

Diminishing Teacher Prejudice

Most educators may agree that inner-city schools are inadequate but disputes continue as to the cause. For those who trace the failure syndrome to social deprivation, it is clearly a matter of deficient nurture, an environment of negative influence during a child's formative years. The opposing view is convinced that blame must reside with members of the school staff whose middle-class orientation and consequent prejudice form the primary obstacle slum children face in their quest to obtain an adequate education. In his review of research, Passow describes the result of culture clash when teachers misunderstand children, when racial bias and stereotypic thinking prevail.

There is conclusive evidence that social origin tends to affect teacher attitude. Whereas Negro teachers, most of whom are reared in homes of low income, tend to view the inner-city child as cooperative, ambitious, fun-loving, and happy, white teachers of middle-class backgrounds see the same children as lazy, rebellious, and high strung. And, since estimates have it that 95 per cent of all teachers come from the middle class, it is not difficult to understand why so much class time is spent in trying to reorient the child of poverty. Passow presents findings which imply that inner-city Negroes receive perhaps only from one-third to one-half as much exposure to learning in the classroom as children from more favored homes. Yet, the amount of work and effort teachers require varies inversely with the pupil's social class. It follows that with less time to learn in school and little instructional assistance at home, retardation is probable.

Wide differences appear to exist between the standard for excellence established in schools of disparate environments. Pupils considered outstanding in the inner city achieve less well than do their suburban age mates who obtain average grades. This over-evaluation of progress for the disadvantaged may appear humane at the time, but later, in situations calling for competition between students of all income groups, the damage to self-concept and aspiration is incalculable. Some would defend their capitulation to low standards by stating the intent to avoid undue criticism, appearing vindictive or prejudiced by assigning numerous grades of failure. But guidance cannot occur if pupils are mislead about either their performance or their promise.

For most beginners an inner-city assignment is perceived as an undesirable ritual of initiation one is expected to endure. In comparing the white teachers who remain in these institutions with white teachers who leave, it comes out that stayers more often appear rooted and unwilling to face the unknown of a new job; they enjoy the autonomy and freedom from outside interferences like the home or administration; and they more often express altruism and loyalty to the principal. But simply remaining or surviving in the school setting is not the same thing as being successful. Apparently many potentially good teachers are lost to the inner city because working conditions there are unacceptable to them. In the main these conditions can be altered by more ample provision of materials, smaller class size, fewer non-instructional tasks, and better support by the administration.

But the essential change that compatibility requires is an improved teacher understanding of the lower-class culture. To accept rejection and hostility without returning them, to provide rules to which these children can adjust, rewards they are willing to pursue, tasks which allow them to demonstrate the strengths gained from their homes—these are the needed mechanisms for change. Passow reminds us that we who train teachers have the task of modifying deleterious attitudes toward the poor by mounting a program of teacher education in which students can see first-hand the problem, its causes, the tenable alternatives for resolution and the professional's responsibility in effecting progress.

Motivating the Slow Learner

Slow learners can be found in schools which serve neighborhoods of every income level. However, whereas their incidence of 18 per cent in the general population means that teachers typically can expect four or five such pupils in a classroom, Johnson reports that from 80 to 90 per cent of slow learners reflect low socioeconomic background. In terms of relative numbers alone, it seems the inner-city teacher must be more cognizant than others regarding problems slow learners face, their learning potential, rates of growth, methods of instructional accommodation, and likely motivation. Unfortunately, in many school systems administrators have the attitude that the least able teachers should be assigned to the children who find it most difficult to learn.

A number of teacher misconceptions regarding the slow learner have been translated into procedures and instructional programs that act to impede pupil gain. For example, one common belief is that slow learners, given enough time and drill, can learn as much and to the same degree as the normal child. Somehow they can catch up and be brought up to grade level if the proper remedial programs are offered and the right kind of pressures induced. Yet Johnson points out that slow learners, who ordinarily score between one and two standard deviations below the mean IQ, can at best be expected to progress from 75 to 90 per cent of the rate prescribed by standards reflected in the courses of study, curricula, and textbooks. Perceiving slow learners as disinterested in school, possessing a short span of attention, and destined to become discipline-truant problems, some educators have favored archaic institutional responses such as increasing the length of school day by keeping these children after hours, increasing their school life by failing them, or increasing the amount of required practice and assigned homework. That none of these techniques is very successful is apparent from the number of slow learners who leave school and from their reported attitudes toward educational curricula and its teachers.

Among the major considerations required for planning an adequate program are the individual's rate of intellectual development and his learning characteristics. It is imperative to recognize that slow learners will be ready for school about one year later than other children and their final level of skill development cannot be expected to exceed the standards of junior high school. Incidentally, the junior high school level of attainment approximates that required for most semi-skilled and skilled jobs. As the slow learner is faced with a limited prospect, it is imperative that the school help him learn to as near his level of ability as possible, for unlike more able persons who can get by without performing at capacity, he must use all he has if he is not to become a social misfit, an economic dependent. This fact underlines the importance of his motivation. Johnson is of the opinion that lessons in content areas can be more meaningful if focused on the proximate. For example, in the social studies, as slow learners tend to be less mobile, less active as citizens, vote less often, and serve their community less than their fellows, it follows that national and international events should be de-emphasized in deference to spending more time in studying the community, its agencies, and the responsibilities of its citizens.

There are no unique methods for obtaining success with slow learners. However, evidence does suggest they do better if taught directly. That is, while the unit method can be helpful in many ways to most students, its integrative nature often confuses a slow learner who gains little from incidental instruction. Ordinarily the unit method lacks developmental materials; as a result skill and instruction are not systematic. And, systematic instruction is an essential ingredient for the slow learner since his achievement of new skills is contingent upon the mastery of successive steps. For this reason, slow learners profit most by learning to read in a reading class which uses developmental materials. To these children, whose growth deviates more in amount than kind from their peers, life can be satisfying and productive or it can be shallow and without meaning—schools often make the difference.

Discipline: Function or Task?

Teachers newly assigned to schools in disadvantaged neighborhoods admit to being apprehensive and reluctant where discipline is concerned. A number of them who have heard reports of youth crime and malevolence fear that student misbehavior might escalate to disorder and confusion unless dealt with severely from the outset. Ordinarily teachers who hold this attitude adopt the discipline task as a primary goal under the guise of removing obstacles to their instructional success. Others believe that if students can be convinced the teacher is sincere and genuinely interested in them, problems of misbehavior will not arise. Both approaches annually yield a large number of requests for transfer as the one type of teacher grows dissatisfied with his role as a monitor while the other feels that students who seemingly cannot respect learning ought to be tutored by someone else.

Even a brief observation of school conditions reveals why the inner-city teacher feels unprotected. Hunt and Rasof explain there is little parental support when disruptive behavior occurs in the classroom; the children are generally irresponsive to usually effective if not wise threats such as assigning poor grades; most of the pupils are subject to corporal punishment at home but are aware that this mode is prohibited for school staff; and student concept of what is bad and what is good seems distorted. In addition, the advice offered during college days seems ineffectual in retrospect for positive results do not take place simply by "looking at or standing near the offender," by "requesting a parent-teacher conference," or "appealing to good manners and fair play." Often, teachers in need of advice feel they cannot turn to their principal or colleagues since to seek help in matters of discipline is construed as an admission of failure because it is generally believed the good teacher can handle his children. Under these conditions, the mental health of an instructor, and in turn his efficiency, are adversely affected.

Apart from a need for improved support by the administration in dealing with culpably misbehaving youngsters and the need for a more realistic type of preparation in college, enabling one to respond wisely to egregious action, Hunt and Rasof emphasize the need for those already on the job to better interpret undesirable patterns of behavior. As most of poverty's children have little training in the social skills which predicate getting along with others, it follows that relationships may be punctuated by disputes which take the form of bickering and assault. This requires change more than punishment. The sullen demeanor and curt remarks of these boys and girls should not be construed as a personal affront by the teacher for this pupil reaction is characteristic of their every association with adults. Then too, unaccustomed to maintaining silence for other people, it is natural for these youngsters to forget the rules or fail to realize the importance of working quietly, to refrain from talking during the study period. Of course, children cannot be excused for all these things, but to understand the cause for such behavior can tend to mediate teacher response in the direction of profit for everyone concerned.

A broad suggestion offered by Hunt and Rasoff is to create a failure-free setting in which the reasons for misbehavior are reduced. Children then find themselves able to succeed within realistic limits and no longer have use for the vent of academic frustration. This can occur if we daily allow each student to experience success by adjusting standards to meet individual abilities, using new media and instructional innovations, and encouraging ever higher levels of aspiration. While discipline is important in every classroom, its emphasis should be on prevention, a by-product of fair classroom management. When students realize a teacher is firm but equitable in his relationships they will spread the word and establish his reputation for the future. This is not to say that instances of student upset will never occur but that the number of cases will decline. Although Hunt and Rasof insist no universals can be prescribed, they remind us common sense dictates that we seek the cause of misbehavior, that anger be absent from our response, and that consistency be our policy. Certainly no child should be subject to ridicule and sarcasm; no child should be subject to reprimand before his peers; no child should be provided an audience for a tantrum; no child should be backed into a position from which he cannot extricate himself with honor—no child should be denied understanding.

Reaching the Parents

The constricted life space of deprived youngsters has prompted a search for new ways in which parents can be enlisted to support the learning process and reduce obstacles to education that are engendered in the home. Fusco documents several investigations which show the crucial differences in cognitive behavior and motivation that typically distinguish between middle- and low-income children upon entering school. Whereas the preparation of middle-class boys and girls is characterized by an emphasis on problem solving, inquiry, and mental process, this foundation is less likely to occur in lower-class homes where physical behavior is accentuated, where being good in school receives greater stress than doing well. The problem of home-school conjunctive effort continues into the upper elementary and secondary grades, for there important decisions are made regarding academic problems and vocational choice. In the absence of joint venture, both institutions are likely to fail in their responsibility to children.

Recognizing the need for a working alliance between parents and teachers at every stage of child development, Fusco suggests a variety of strategies that have proven successful in large school systems. The preschool approaches, all designed to help families ready their children for the elementary grades, include examples of: A Detroit nursery program in which mothers learn how to share information and program simple tasks by serving as teacher assistants; a Baltimore experiment for teaching parents about child development through their observation of classrooms; a liaison plan in Philadelphia which employs an esteemed lay person to serve as a coordinator between home and school, to interpret educational policies for parents, and to provide teachers with information about the family.

Many parents of children in elementary and secondary grades are reluctant to participate in conferences because their own dissatisfying academic experience has served to alienate them from teachers. Somehow these mothers and fathers must be convinced that school personnel sincerely desire to assist the child. To accomplish this bond, one Detroit staff has initiated a "special class contract" stipulating an intent to offer remedial classes for children who need it, subject to certain assurances of psychological support by the home. Other school plans are designed to incorporate the assistance of parents who find a personal conference situation uncomfortable. For example, in a Detroit junior high school, parents are invited as a group to discuss problems of adolescence and to consider ways by which their boys and girls can better prepare for high school. The prospect of using this non-threatening group orientation for conferences is shown in the statistic that of those attending the meetings in Detroit, over 90 per cent were not involved in any other school activity.

To develop better understanding of the values which accrue from participation in cultural activities outside the school, a Philadelphia junior high school plans Saturday trips with parents to farms, parks, libraries, and places of historical interest. During the briefing sessions, parents are told what to expect in transit and at the destination so that they can better answer children's questions and feel more secure as guides. Fusco found that since experiencing firsthand the many free and inexpensive sources of recreation and interest in the community and its adjacent areas, a large number of inner-city parents have themselves begun planning for family outings and trips. Similarly, in Chicago, Baltimore, and Detroit, there are schools which arrange free and inexpensive ventures so that parents and children can attend functions together. Some schools also compile helpful guides to community resources in health, recreation and education. That parents not abdicate their leadership in the home is a necessity. If the school does its part in assisting parents, then leadership can be wiser in its direction and more likely to succeed.

In almost every case the authors of this volume offer a question which presses for a reply—What of the poor? In the final analysis, each of us must answer the question for himself as each of us has his own answer. Consider this: Unless we the educated can read our responsibility, perhaps ours is the greater form of illiteracy.

Bibliography

Allport, Gordon W. "Attitudes," in *A Handbook of Social Psychology*, ed. Carl A. Murchison. Worchester, Mass.: Clark University Press, 1935, p. 810.

————. "The Normality of Prejudgment," in *The Nature of Prejudice*, Garden City, N.J.: Doubleday & Co., Inc., 1958, pp. 17-27.

Altus, G. T. "Some Correlates of the Davis-Eells Test," *Journal of Consulting Psychology*, XX, No. 3 (1956), 227-32.

Anderson, K. G. *Creativity Is*. Unpublished manuscript. Berkeley, Calif., 1964.

Ausubel, David P., and Pearl Ausubel. "Ego Development Among Segregated Negro Children," in *Education in Depressed Areas*, ed. A. Harry Passow. New York: Teachers College, Columbia University, 1963, p. 109.

Becker, Howard S. "Social-Class Variations in Teacher-Pupil Relationships," *Journal of Educational Sociology*, XXV (April 1952a), 452, 462.

————. "The Career of the Chicago Public Schoolteacher," *American Journal of Sociology*, LVII, No. 5 (March 1952b), 470-77.

Bernstein, Basil. "Social Class and Linguistic Development," in *Economy, Education, and Society*, eds. A. H. Halsey, Jean Floud, and C. Arnold Anderson. Glencoe, Ill.: Free Press of Glencoe, Inc., 1961.

Biber, Barbara. "Integration of Mental Health Principles in the School Setting," in *Prevention of Mental Disorders in Children*, ed. G. Caplan. New York: Basic Books, Inc., Publishers, 1961.

————. "Premature Structuring as a Deterrent to Creativity," *American Journal of Orthopsychiatry*, Vol. 29, No. 2 (April 1959), 280-90.

————. "Aspects of a Learning-Teaching Paradigm Based on Interaction of Intellectual and Affective Processes," in *Behavioral Science Frontiers in Education*, eds. W. G. Hollister and E. M. Bower. New York: John Wiley & Sons, Inc., 1965.

Bloom, B. S. "The Effect of Variations in Environment on Intelligence," in *Stability and Change in Human Characteristics*. New York: John Wiley & Sons, Inc., 1964, pp. 68-76.

————. *Taxonomy of Educational Objectives: The Classification of Educational Objectives*. New York: David McKay Co., Inc., 1956.

————, A. Davis, and R. Hess. *Compensatory Education for Cultural Deprivation*. New York: Holt, Rinehart & Winston, Inc., 1965, pp. 12-19.

Bowman, Paul, and Charles V. Matthews. *The Motivations of Youth for Leaving School*. Project 200, Cooperative Research Program, U.S. Office of Education, 1958.

Brickell, Henry M. *Organizing New York State for Educational Changes*. Albany, New York: The University of the State of New York, State Education Department, 1961.

Bronfenbrenner, U. "The Changing American Child—A Speculative Analysis," *Merrill-Palmer Quarterly*, VII, No. 2 (April 1961), 73-84.

Brookover, W., S. Thomas, and A. Patterson. "Self Concept of Ability and School Achievement," *Sociology of Education*, Vol. 37 (Spring 1964), 271-78.

Bruner, Jerome Seymour. "Learning and Thinking," *Harvard Educational Review*, Vol. 29, No. 3 (Summer 1959), 184-92.

————. *The Process of Education*. Cambridge, Mass.: Harvard University Press, 1960.

Burkhart, R. C., and G. Bernheim. *Object Question Test Manual*. University Park, Pa.: Department of Art Education, Pennsylvania State University, 1963.

Burton, William H. "Education and Social Class in the United States," *Harvard Educational Review*, XXIII, No. 4 (Fall 1953), 243-256.

Carricker, William R. (ed.). *Role of the School in the Prevention of Juvenile Delinquency*. Research Symposium, U.S. Office of Education. Washington, D.C.: U.S. Government Printing Office, 1963.

Clark, Kenneth B. *Dark Ghetto: Dilemmas of Social Power*. New York: Harper and Row, Publishers, 1965, pp. 128-9.

————. "Educational Stimulation of Racially Disadvantaged Children," in *Education in Depressed Areas*, ed. A. Harry Passow. New York: Teachers College, Columbia University, 1963, p. 157.

Cloward, Richard A., and James A. Jones. "Social Class: Educational Attitudes and Participation," in *Education in Depressed Areas*, ed. A. Harry Passow. New York: Teachers College, Columbia University, 1963, pp. 190-216.

Combs, Arthur W. "A Perceptual View of the Adequate Personality," in *Perceiving, Behaving, Becoming*, ed. Arthur W. Combs. Washington, D.C.: Association for Supervision and Curriculum Development, National Education Association, 1962, pp. 50-64.

Conant, James Bryant. *Slums and Suburbs*. New York: McGraw-Hill Book Co., Inc., 1961.

Conner, James. "The Teacher in a World of Increasing Impersonal Relationships," in *Mental Health and Achievement*, eds. E. Paul Torrance and Robert D. Strom. New York: John Wiley & Sons, 1965, pp. 174-181.

Davis, Allison. *Social Class Influences upon Learning*. Cambridge, Mass.: Harvard University Press, 1948.

————. "Society, the School and the Culturally Deprived Student," in *Improving English Skills of Culturally Different Youth in Large Cities*, eds. Arno Jewett, Joseph Mersand, and Doris V. Gunderson. Washington, D.C.: U.S. Government Printing Office, 1964, p. 15.

Deutsch, Martin. *Minority Group and Class Status as Related to Social and Personality Factors in Scholastic Achievement*. Ithaca, New York: Society for Applied Anthropology, Monograph No. 2, 1960, pp. 3, 23.

————, A. Maliver, B. Brown, and E. Cherry. *The Communication and Information in the Elementary Classroom*. New York: Institute for Developmental Studies, Department of Psychiatry, New York Medical College, Cooperative Research Project No. 808, 1964b.

————, J. Fishman, L. Kogan, R. North, and M. Whitman. "Guidelines for Testing Minority Group Children," *Journal of Social Issues*, XX, No. 2 (1964a), 129-45.

Downing, Gertrude, Robert W. Edgar, Albert J. Harris, Leonard Kornberg, and Helen F. Storen. *The Preparation of Teachers for Schools in Culturally Deprived Neighborhoods*. Flushing, New York: The BRIDGE Project, Cooperative Research Project No. 935, Queens College of the City University of New York, 1965, pp. 52-54.

Educational Policies Commission. *Education and the Disadvantaged American*. Washington, D.C.: National Education Association, 1962.

Eisenberg, Leon. "Strengths of the Inner-City Child," *Baltimore Bulletin of Education*, XLI, No. 2 (1963-64), 10, 16.

Ellison, Ralph. "What These Children Are Like," in *Education of the Deprived and Segregated*. New York: Seminar on Education for Culturally Different Youth, Cooperative Research Project No. G-021, Bank Street College of Education, 1965, p. 47.

Erikson, Erik. "The Problem of Ego Identity," in *Identity and Anxiety*, eds. M. R. Stein, A. J. Vidich, and D. M. White. Glencoe, Ill.: Free Press of Glencoe, Inc., 1960.

Estvan, Frank J., and Elizabeth W. Estvan. *The Child's World—His Social Perception*. New York: G. P. Putnam's Sons, 1959.

Featherstone, William B. *Teaching the Slow Learner*. New York: Bureau of Publications, Teachers College, Columbia University, 1951.

Festinger, L. "Wish, Expectation, and Group Standards as Factors Influencing Level of Aspiration," *Journal of Abnormal and Social Psychology*, 37 (April 1942), 184-200.

Freedman, Philip I. "Racial Attitudes as a Factor in Teacher Education for the Deprived Child." Unpublished paper, Hunter College.

Frymier, Jack R. *The Nature of Educational Method*. Columbus, Ohio: Charles E. Merrill Books, Inc., 1965.

Fuchs, Estelle S. *Pickets at the Gates*. New York: Project TRUE, Hunter College of the City University of New York, 1965, pp. 3-8.

Fusco, Gene C. *School-Home Partnership*. Washington, D.C.: U.S. Government Printing Office, OE 31008, Bulletin No. 20, 1964.

Gold, Milton J. *Education of the Intellectually Gifted*. Columbus, Ohio: Charles E. Merrill Books, Inc., 1965.

Goldberg, Miriam L. "Adapting Teacher Style to Pupil Differences: Teachers for Disadvantaged Children," *Merrill-Palmer Quarterly*, X, No. 2 (1964), 167-68.

————. "Methods and Materials for Educationally Disadvantaged Youth." A paper prepared for the Post-Doctoral Seminar of the College of Education, The Ohio State University, Columbus, Ohio, October 1964.

Good, Warren R. "Misconceptions About Intelligence Testing," *University of Michigan School of Education Bulletin*, XXV (May 1954), 117-20.

Gottlieb, David. "Teaching and Students: The Views of Negro and White Teachers." Unpublished paper, Michigan State University, August 1963, pp. 2-3, 9.

Hamacheck, Donald. "Studies in Self-Concept Suggest Changes in Teaching Approach," *Michigan Journal of Secondary Education*, Vol. 5, No. 2 (Winter 1964), 7-14.

Hanson, Doris Elizabeth. "Home Economists in Overseas Work." Doctoral dissertation, Teachers College, Columbia University, New York, 1964.

Harlem Youth Opportunities Unlimited, Inc. *Youth in the Ghetto: A Study of the Consequences of Powerlessness*. New York: HARYOU, 1964, p. 204.

Haubrich, Vernon F. "Teachers for Big-City Schools," in *Education in Depressed Areas*, ed. A. Harry Passow. New York: Teachers College, Columbia University, 1963, p. 246.

Havighurst, Robert, Paul Bowman, *et al*. *Growing up in River City*. New York: John Wiley & Sons, Inc., 1962.

Henderson, George. "Raising the Levels of Aspiration of Children Whose Parents Are Receiving Public Subsidy: A Pilot Project." Detroit Urban League, 1962.

Hess, Robert D., and V. Shipman. "Early Experience and the Socialization of Cognitive Modes in Children," *Child Development*, Vol. 36, No. 4 (December 1965).

Hillson, Henry T., and Florence C. Myers. *The Demonstration Guidance Project, 1957-1962: Pilot Program for Higher Horizons*. New York: George Washington High School, Board of Education, 1963.

Hollingshead, August B. *Elmtown's Youth*. New York: John Wiley & Sons, Inc., 1949.

Horrocks, John E. "Culture Free Tests of Intelligence," in *Assessment of Behavior*. Columbus, Ohio: Charles E. Merrill Books, Inc., 1964, pp. 271-96.

Hymes, James L., Jr. *A Pound of Prevention*. New York: Teachers Service Committee on the Emotional Needs of Children, 1947.

Ingram, Christine P. *Education of the Slow-Learning Child*. 3d ed. New York: The Ronald Press Co., 1960.

Jenkins, Gladys Gardner. *Helping Children Reach Their Potential*. Chicago: Scott, Foresman & Co., 1961.

Jersild, Arthur J. *In Search of Self*. New York: Bureau of Publications, Teachers College, Columbia University, 1960.

Johnson, G. Orville. *Education for the Slow Learners*. Englewood Cliffs, N.J.: Prentice-Hall, Inc., 1963.

————. *The Slow Learner—A Second-Class Citizen?* Syracuse, New York: Syracuse University Press, 1962.

Johnson, Wendell. *Your Most Enchanted Listener*. New York: Harper & Row, Publishers, 1956, p. 75.

Jordan, Thomas E. *The Mentally Retarded*, 2d. ed. Columbus, Ohio: Charles E. Merrill Books, Inc., 1966.

Kaufman, Bel. *Up the Down Staircase*. Englewood Cliffs, N.J.: Prentice-Hall, Inc., 1964.

Kelley, Earl C. "The Fully Functioning Self," in *Perceiving, Behaving, Becoming,* ed. Arthur W. Combs. Washington, D.C.: Association for Supervision and Curriculum Development, National Education Association, 1962 (Yearbook), pp. 9-20.

Kephart, Newell C. *The Slow Learner in the Classroom*. Columbus, Ohio: Charles E. Merrill Books, Inc., 1960.

Kirk, Samuel A. *Teaching Reading to Slow Learning Children*. Boston: Houghton Mifflin Co., 1940.

Kornberg, Leonard. "Meaningful Teachers for Alienated Children," in *Education in Depressed Areas,* ed. A. Harry Passow. New York: Teachers College, Columbia University, 1963, pp. 265, 274.

Lohman, Joseph D. *Cultural Patterns of Differentiated Youth: A Manual for Teachers in Marginal Schools*. Berkeley, Calif.: University of California, n.d., pp. 25, 83-84.

Love, M. I., and S. Beach. "Performance of Children on the Davis-Eells Games and Other Measures of Ability," *Journal of Consulting Psychology,* XXI, No. 1 (1957), 29-32.

Mead, George H. *Mind, Self and Society*. Chicago: University of Chicago Press, 1937.

Medinnus, Gene R. "The Development of a Parent Attitude Toward Education Scale," *Journal of Educational Research,* 56 (1962), 100-103.

Mental Health Project Grant #535, National Institute of Mental Health. Progress report available from Community Studies, Inc., 2300 Holmes, Kansas City, Missouri.

Miller, Harry L. "The Effect of Information on Student Beliefs about the Slum School." New York: Hunter College Project TRUE, 1963, pp. 1-2.

Morgan, James N. *Income and Welfare in the United States*. New York: McGraw-Hill Book Co., Inc., 1962.

National Education Association. "High School Methods with Slow Learners," *National Education Association Research Bulletin,* XXI, No. 3 (October 1943), 60-87.

Panel on Educational Research and Development of the President's Science Advisory Committee, *Innovation and Experiment in Education*. Washington, D.C.: U.S. Government Printing Office, 1964, p. 30.

Pascal, Blaise. "Pensées," in *Book of Quotations,* ed. Franklin P. Adams. New York: Funk & Wagnalls Co., Inc. 1952, p. 418.

Passow, A. Harry. "Instructional Content for Depressed Urban Centers:

Problems and Approaches." A paper prepared for the Post-Doctoral Seminar of the College of Education, The Ohio State University, October 1964.

————. "Teachers for Depressed Areas," in *Education in Depressed Areas*, ed. A. Harry Passow. New York: Teachers College, Columbia University, 1963, p. 238.

Peck, Robert F., and Robert J. Havighurst. *The Psychology of Character Development*. New York: John Wiley & Sons, Inc., 1960.

Redl, Fritz, and George V. Sheviakob. *Discipline for Today's Children and Youth*. Washington, D.C.: Association for Supervision and Curriculum Development, National Education Association, 1956.

Reissman, Leonard. "Levels of Aspiration and Social Class," *American Sociological Review*, 18 (June 1953), 233-42.

Riessman, Frank. *The Culturally Deprived Child*. New York: Harper and Row, Publishers, 1962.

————. "The Culturally Deprived Child: A New View," in *Mental Health and Achievement*, eds. E. Paul Torrance and Robert D. Strom. New York: John Wiley & Sons, Inc., 1965a, pp. 312-19.

————. "The Lessons of Poverty," *American Education*, Vol. 1, No. 2 (February 1965b).

————, Jerome Cohen, and Arthur Pearl (eds.). *Mental Health of the Poor*. Glencoe, Ill.: Free Press of Glencoe, Inc., 1964.

Rivlin, Harry N. "Teachers for the Schools in Our Big Cities." A paper prepared for the University of Pennsylvania Schoolmen's Week Program, October 12, 1962, p. 7.

Saltzman, Henry. "The Community in the Urban Setting," in *Education in Depressed Areas*, ed. A. Harry Passow. New York: Teachers College, Columbia University, 1963, pp. 322-31.

Schreiber, D., B. Kaplan, and R. D. Strom. *Dropout Studies: Design and Conduct*. Washington, D.C.: National Education Association, 1965.

Sexton, Patricia C. *Education and Income*. New York: The Viking Press, 1961, p. 79.

Smilansky, Sarah. "Evaluation of Early Education," *UNESCO Educational Studies and Documents*, No. 42 (1961), 8-17.

Smiley, Marjorie. "Research and Its Implications," in *"Improving English Skills of Culturally Different Youth in Large Cities*, eds. Arno Jewett, Joseph Mersand, and Doris V. Gunderson. Washington, D.C.: U.S. Government Printing Office, 1964, pp. 53-54.

Stendler, Celia B. *Children of Brasstown*. Urbana, Ill.: University of Illinois Press, 1949.

Strom, Robert D. "Education: Key to Economic Equality for the Negro," *Journal of Negro Education*, Vol. 34, #4 (Fall 1965b), pp. 463-66.

————. "Preparation and Recruitment of Teachers," in *Teaching in the Slum School*. Columbus, Ohio: Charles E. Merrill Books, Inc., 1965a, pp. 30-47.

————. *The Tragic Migration*. Washington, D.C.: The Department of Home Economics, National Education Association, 1964.

Sullivan, Harry S. *Conceptions of Modern Psychiatry*. 2d ed. New York: W. W. Norton & Co., Inc. 1953.

Taylor, Calvin. "A Tentative Description of the Creative Individual," in *Human Variability and Learning*, ed. Walter B. Waetjen. Washington, D.C.: Association for Supervision and Curriculum Development, National Education Association, 1961, p. 65.

Theobold, Robert. "Poverty in an Era of Overabundance." Speech delivered in Cooper Union, New York City, November 3, 1964. Forum Series: *Great Issues of 1964-65*, broadcast over National Education Radio Network Station WNYC.

Toby, Jackson. "Orientation to Education as a Factor in School Maladjustment of Lower Class Children," *Social Factors*, XXXV (March 1957).

Torrance, E. Paul. "Asking Provocative Questions," *The Instructor*, Vol. 74. No. 2 (October 1964b), pp. 35, 72, 78.

————. *Guiding Creative Talent*. Englewood Cliffs, N.J.: Prentice-Hall, Inc., 1962.

————. *Gifted Children in the Classroom*. New York: The Macmillan Company, 1965c.

————. "Introduction: Man's Mental Operations," in *Constructive Behavior: Stress, Personality and Mental Health*. Belmont, Calif.: Wadsworth Publishing Co., Inc., 1965a, pp. 187-91.

————. *Rewarding Creative Behavior: Experiments in Classroom Creativity*. Englewood Cliffs, N.J.: Prentice-Hall, Inc., 1965b.

————, and R. Gupta. *Programmed Experiences in Creative Thinking*. Minneapolis: Bureau of Educational Research, University of Minnesota, 1964a.

U.S. Department of Health, Education, and Welfare, Office of Education. *Teaching Rapid and Slow Learners in High Schools*. Washington, D.C.: Bulletin No. 5, 1954.

Warner, W. Lloyd, Robert J. Havighurst, and Martin B. Loeb. *Who Shall be Educated?* New York: Harper & Row, Publishers, 1944.

Watson, Goodwin B. (ed.). *No Room at the Bottom.* Washington, D.C.: National Education Association, 1964.

Wattenberg, William. *Relationship of School Experience to Delinquency.* Washington, D.C.: U.S. Office Cooperative Research Project #201, U.S. Government Printing Office, 1959.

Wayson, William W. "Sources of Satisfaction in Slum Schools." Unpublished preliminary report, Syracuse University, n.d.

Wheeler, Robert H. "Progress Report of the Special Scholarship Program." Kansas City, Mo.: Department of Guidance, Public Schools, 1963.

Will, Patricia Phinney. "A Study of the Effects of Possible Emotional Disturbance on the Creative Behavior of a Group of Delinquent Girls." Unpublished M.A. research paper, University of Minnesota, 1964.

Wilson, Alan B. "Social Stratification and Academic Achievement," in *Education in Depressed Areas,* ed. A. Harry Passow. New York: Teachers College, Columbia University, 1963, p. 234.

Wolf, Eleanor P., and Leo Wolf. "Sociological Perspective on the Education of Culturally Deprived Children," *School Review,* LXX, No. 4 (Winter 1962), 381-82.

Zacharias, Jerrold. "Learning by Teaching." Speech delivered at the 1965 White House Conference on Education. Washington, D.C., July 1965.

INDEXES

Index of Names

Index of Subjects